JESUS
IN
CHRISTIAN DEVOTION AND CONTEMPLATION

Religious Experience Series

Edward J. Malatesta, S.J., General Editor

Volumes in Preparation:

      Paths to Contemplation

      Contemplation in the Greek Fathers

      The Theology of Contemplation

Religious Experience Series

Volume I

Jesus

in

Christian Devotion and Contemplation

by
Irénée Noye, S.S., Charles Kannengiesser, S.J.,
Paul Agaesse, S.J., Jacques Hourlier, O.S.B.,
André Rayez, S.J., Tomas de la Cruz, O.C.D.

Translated by
Paul J. Oligny, O.F.M.

With a Preface by
Edward Malatesta, S.J.

ABBEY PRESS
St. Meinrad, Indiana 47577
1974

348
Ma J

The present work is a translation of the article "Humanité du Christ (Dévotion et contemplation)" which first appeared in the *Dictionnaire de Spiritualité*, Paris, Beauchesne, 1969, vol. 8, cols. 1033-1108.

© 1974 by Edward Malatesta, S.J.
Library of Congress Catalog Card Number: 73-94170
ISBN: 0-87029-025-8
Printed in the United States of America

Preface

by Edward Malatesta, S.J.

The story of every person's life is ultimately the story of a relationship with Jesus Christ. All of us have been created through Him, in Him, and for Him (Jn 1:3; Col 1:15-16), and all of us have been reconciled through Him to the Father (2 Cor 5:18-20; Col 1:20). His is the only name in which all can find lasting happiness (Acts 4:12); He is the unique and indispensable foundation of God's saving work among us (1 Cor 3:10-15; see Mt 7:24-27).

It is the privilege and the joy of us who are Christians to know the mystery of God's design in Jesus Christ, to recognize Him as the Alpha and Omega of all history (Ap 22:13). It is our responsibility and our duty to articulate to all men, in a language they can understand, the meaning of Jesus Christ for their lives. He is indeed already in the hearts of everyone as the source of all the beauty and goodness expressed in human living. Ours it is to lead all men to discover Him there.

To the degree that we take seriously this aspect of our Christian vocation, we realize the delicacy and the urgency of our mission. Unfortunately a radical Bultmannian mentality still persists in some Christian milieux—including Roman Catholic ones—with the result that the knowable content of the life of Jesus of Nazareth is reduced practically to a cipher. Often a hypercritical approach to the study of the gospels, which in the last analysis is contrary to good scientific method, leads to a harvest of mutually contradictory hypotheses and a chronic scepticism regarding the possibility of any clear knowledge whatever about Jesus. The personality of Jesus thus becomes formless; an intimate relationship with Him becomes impossible.

On the brighter side, New Testament scholarship such as that of C. H. Dodd, J. Guillet, and J. Jeremias[1] intends to use the best critical methods in order to deepen the Christian's knowledge of his Lord and so enrich his daily faith-encounter with Him. This encounter does in fact take many forms, and it would be an unfortunate misrepresentation and mutilation of Christian experience to fail properly to evaluate or generously to live any one of them. The manner in which these several facets blend in one's personal relationship with Christ depends upon the kind and measure of the various gifts of nature and grace given to each person, and upon the individual's response to these gifts. We will attempt here briefly to mention what seems to us three of the most important forms of communion with the risen Jesus experienced by Christians who try seriously to live their faith.

The liturgy, especially the celebration of the Eucharist, but also of the other sacraments and of the Divine Office, offers a privileged means of interpersonal communion with Jesus who is present in the Word which is proclaimed, in the sacrament which is offered and received, in the assembly which prays and sings together, in the ministers who preside over the celebration.[2] The liturgy renders present to us not only the Paschal Mystery of Jesus, but also the other mysteries of His life which are celebrated throughout the liturgical year and proclaimed in the Scripture readings. The risen Lord who is present to the worshipping community, who indeed is *the* leader of the prayer it addresses in His Name and in His Spirit to the Father, possesses in Himself even now all the qualities which he manifested during His life upon earth, all the experiences He underwent while He was visibly present among men. The holiness of Jesus, perfect God and perfect man, is communicated to us, the members of His Mystical Body, when we celebrate His mysteries in the liturgy. The Holy Spirit, "first Gift to those who believe," is especially active during the liturgical celebration. He who is the bond of love between the Father and the Son joins the faithful to Jesus, to the Father, and to one another. The disciples of Jesus bring to each liturgy the store of knowledge of Him which they have assimilated from many sources. The Holy Spirit actualizes this knowledge and increases it by a new encounter with the risen Lord in faith and love.

If the liturgy represents the most perfect form of Christian prayer, it is not the only one. Other forms of prayer, both private and collective,[3] offer us many means of personal communion with Jesus. Normally speaking, the Scriptures, and especially the gospels, provide the starting-point, the normative inspiration, and the constant nourishment of Christian prayer. Since the Word of God was composed under the inspiration of the Holy Spirit, the first rule of an integral Christian interpretation is that it be read "in the same Spirit by whom it was written."[4] The Holy Spirit therefore is the incomparable Exegete of the Scriptures. He alone can produce in the minds and hearts of the disciples of Jesus His sentiments (Phil 2:5); He alone can join the bride to her bridegroom, for He it is who inspires the desire for union with Him (Ap 22:17). When speaking of the contemplation of the Scriptures as a means of encountering the risen Jesus, we should remember the words which conclude the Fourth Gospel: "But there are also many other things which Jesus did; were every one of them to be written, I suppose that the world itself could not contain the books that would be written" (Jn 21:25). The personality of Jesus is richer than what even the inspired authors wrote about Him. He outdistances the experiences of Him enjoyed by His saints, and all their expressions about Him. The role of the gospels therefore is *neither* to present the reflections of a community which have no basis in the historical personality of Jesus, *nor* to provide an exhaustive description of Jesus and His actions. Rather, by placing us in communion with the inspired witnesses to Jesus and by generating in us faith in and love toward Him, they offer us the milieu of an encounter with Him which both embraces the content and surpasses the limitations of His historical life, of the experience and expression of the first witnesses and of ourselves. The gospels are limited documents, and no one was more aware of this than their human authors. The ultimate purpose of these texts therefore is to introduce us to the risen Jesus who dwells in our hearts. To the degree that we know the Jesus portrayed in the gospels, we shall recognize the risen one present within us. And our experience of communion with the risen Jesus will cause the words of the gospels to ring as so many echoes of intuitions we have already known.

The encounter with Jesus in the liturgy and in other forms

of prayer naturally tends toward and is completed by encounter with Him in all our brothers and sisters. Jesus is present and reveals Himself in every person because by reason of His Incarnation He, the most beautiful of the sons of men, is reflected in the perfections that every person possesses. Every child of God is related to the only-begotten Son; the dignity and destiny of each derives ultimately from Jesus, Creator, Saviour, and Lord of all of us.

Jesus is present to each of us in our human frailty and sinfulness as our advocate and our expiation (1 Jn 2:1-2), and our healer (Acts 10:38). The awareness of sin in ourselves or in others should express itself not in masochistic self-hatred or in pharisaical disdain of others, but rather in the humble recognition of the need we have and in heartfelt compassion for the need others have of the merciful forgiveness which Jesus offered to all He met during His life, and which He continues to offer to all men through His Paschal Mystery. Sin by expressing humanity's need for a Saviour occasions our turning toward Jesus, the unique Saviour of us all.

Finally Jesus is present and reveals Himself in the little ones: in the suffering and the poor of every kind. Indeed, in unequivocal and ever-challenging terms He chose to identify Himself with the most humble and the most needy (Mt 25:31-46; 10:42; Mk 9:37). His very Incarnation was the expression of a gift of self which will elicit our admiration for all eternity (Phil 2:6-7). His entire life and ministry among us was under the sign of humility and meekness (Mt 11:29). His Passion and death represent the ultimate in self-giving (Phil 2:8; Heb 5:8). Because He experienced within Himself the utmost abasement, all of those who are diminished and needy in any way mirror His mystery in a manner for which He expressed His predilection.

These three ways of encountering Jesus Christ—in the liturgy, in other forms of prayer, in all our brothers and sisters—far from being mutually exclusive, compenetrate and enrich one another. They are really three aspects, among many, of meeting Jesus which in their effects are not limited to precise moments of time; they are co-present to one another. The grace of the liturgical encounter, for example, carries over into private prayer, into various expressions of group prayer, into our daily converse with others, while the graces of these latter come to bear upon our celebration of the liturgy.

What is decisive is the meeting with Jesus, for otherwise there is no Christianity. What is essential is "the surpassing worth of knowing Christ Jesus" (Phil 2:8), our Lord, for otherwise we cannot be His disciples.

The manner in which we live our Christian vocation today should both resemble and differ from the manner in which the followers of Jesus lived this vocation in the past. There should be a similarity, because Jesus Himself "is the same, yesterday, today and forever" (Heb 13:8). Ever present to the successive generations of the Christian era, with the power of His divinity and the perfections of His human nature, He unites and gives direction to all persons, communities, and events. The faithful of every age adore and praise, know, love, and imitate the same Jesus Christ who was born of the Virgin Mary, baptized by John, crucified under Pontius Pilate, and rose on the third day. The faithful of every age encounter this Jesus in the liturgy, in contemplation and in other forms of prayer, and in His members. There is a sameness because the basic responses of the disciple to his Lord remain essentially the same: faith, hope, and love which express themselves in the ongoing conversion toward Jesus, the persevering quest for Him, and the continued discovery of Him.

But there should be differences in the devotion of contemporary Christians to Jesus. The best results that modern Scripture studies can offer should enable us to have a more objective knowledge of the Lord and His disciples, by helping us better to situate them in the context of the Judaism of their times, and by leading us to understand better His total mystery in the light of both the Old and the New Testaments. The de-christianization and secularization of Western society on the one hand, and on the other hand the encounter with non-christian religions in the Orient, Africa, and the Middle East, invite us to discover new traces of Christ (like the *vestigia* recognized by Tradition) in every authentically human aspiration. The intuitions of a Teilhard de Chardin regarding signs of Christ's presence in the complex evolution of human society and of the cosmos itself should be exploited, given adequate expression, and shared widely. Our new awareness of and sensitivity to the injustice and the violence, poverty and moral upheaval which characterize the lives of entire peoples can result in new discoveries of the presence of Jesus in the poor and in the sinful. The aspirations toward peace, brotherhood, and unity which well up in all men to the degree they are moved by an enlightened conscience and good will should enrich our contemplation of Jesus in the perfections which others possess.

The book which these pages preface will, it is hoped, render a twofold service to contemporary Christians. By introducing us to the history of contemplation of and devotion to the humanity of Jesus from Patristic times to the foundation of the Carmelite school of spirituality in the sixteenth century, it can help us discover the depth and extent of our Christian roots. As we pass in review the highlights of the relationship with Jesus which characterized Christians during sixteen centuries, we will be able to examine with a new understanding our own relationship to Him. By learning the *origins* of many forms of Catholic devotion to Jesus with which we have been acquainted and perhaps have practiced (and may still practice with profit), we will be able to evaluate, to use, and to teach these devotions more intelligently, while avoiding the extremes of sentimental enthusiasm and rationalistic disdain.

Secondly, a panoramic vision of that Christian spirit of creativity which resulted in a rich variety of forms of devotion to Jesus might inspire some of us to be creative in our turn, or at least to be informed and prudent judges of the creative efforts of others. In the instructive light of Christian Tradition, *Jesus Christ Superstar* appears as musically clever, perhaps, but certainly as religiously inadequate, while *Godspell* joins hands across the centuries with the best of the *Mystery Plays*.

The following pages will renew our acquaintance with or introduce us to such women as Julian of Norwich, Angela of Foligno, Catherine of Siena, Bridget of Sweden, Gertrude and Mechtild of Helfta, Teresa of Avila, and to such men as John Cassian, Gregory the Great, Anselm, William of Saint-Thierry, Bernard, Aelred of Rievaulx, Francis of Assisi, Bonaventure, Ludolph of Saxony, Richard Rolle, Bernardine of Siena, Meister Eckhart, Henry Suso, John Tauler, John Gerson, Thomas à Kempis, Jan Van Ruysbroeck, Vincent Ferrer, and John of the Cross. If these men and women are better known to us because of the writings they left and the influence they exerted, they represent a vast army of lesser known or totally unknown followers of Jesus whose lives were also centered upon Him. Among rich and poor, among the educated and unlettered, in palace and cottage, in city and country, by hermits and monks, by preachers and cloistered nuns, by clergy and laity, Jesus has been contemplated and proclaimed, adored, loved, and imitated as true God and true man, as the perfect revelation of God's enduring love for man, and as the model and source of man's response of love to God and to his fellows. To consider this aspect of the Christian past is to be challenged in the present and to begin to build for the future.

Direct contact with numerous passages from the writings of the Fathers and from select medieval writers can stimulate us to follow their example of living faith in and ardent love for Jesus. The texts which best witness to the history of the affective contemplation of the mysteries of Jesus contain privileged and normative expressions of Christian wisdom. The thoughts and sentiments which inadequately represent either our faith or the types of affective response it should evoke, warn us of pitfalls to avoid. The excellent studies cited here which situate Christian devotion in its historical and social context can assist us in discovering those devotional forms which best suit our own times.

The sources investigated and cited by the authors of this volume and painstakingly arranged in footnotes by Father Paul Oligny, O.F.M., an accomplished translator, suggest paths of study and reflection which we hope many readers will have the opportunity to pursue.

The millions of young people the world over who have been baptized into the Body of Christ have a privileged opportunity, one unparalleled in history, to discover and to express in new ways, to the other millions who know Him not, "the unsearchable riches of Christ" (Eph 3:8). The new generation is inward, artistic, and sensitive. It prophesies the unity and brotherhood of all men. It sees visions of justice and peace (see Acts 2:17-18; Joel 2:28-29). To those who are disciples of Jesus can be opened the treasures of the Sacred Scriptures in an unprecedented way. They can more easily visit the land where Jesus lived, celebrate in new liturgical forms all the aspects of

His mysteries. They have more possibilities than ever to be led along the paths of Christian contemplation, to the experience of Jesus and His gospel.

Jesus promised that one of the activities of the Paraclete, the Spirit of Truth, would be to teach His disciples all things, to bring to remembrance all that He had been and said and done, and so to lead them into all truth (see Jn 14:26; 16:13). Jesus' promise has been kept. Over the centuries the Holy Spirit has led Christians to intimate friendship with Jesus. Today He is no less active in drawing the brothers and sisters of Jesus through the world "to know Him more clearly, love Him more dearly and follow Him more nearly, day by day." The Spirit is preparing a new chapter in the history of the humanity of Christ in Christian devotion and contemplation, a chapter which will be written by those of us who bear the name of Christ today, and who have the vocation to say to others: "Behold the Lamb of God who takes away the sin of the world. . . . We have found the Messiah . . . Come and see" (Jn 1:29. 36.41.46).

Edward Malatesta, S.J.
Rome
Christmas 1973

Translator's Note

The translator wishes to express his sincere gratitude to Father Brennan A. Connelly, O.F.M., for his painstaking reading of the typescript and for his many valuable suggestions.

Paul J. Oligny, O.F.M.

List of Abbreviations

ACW	Ancient Christian Writers	Westminster, Md.
ANF	Ante-Nicene Fathers	Grand Rapids (reprint)
CF	Cistercian Fathers	Washington, D.C.
DS	*Dictionnaire de Spiritualité*	Paris
FC	Fathers of the Church	New York; Washington, D.C.
NPNF	Nicene and Post-Nicene Fathers	Grand Rapids (reprint)
PL	*Patrologia latina*	Paris
RAM	*Revue d'ascétique et mystique*	Toulouse
SC	*Sources chrétiennes*	Paris

Contents

Introduction

Christians have always been sensitive to everything that had to do with Christ, His historical life, His deeds and actions, and His person. Devotion to the humanity of Christ came about, one might say, spontaneously. It has grown considerably down through the course of the centuries, taking root in worship, meditation, devotions, religious literature, and the arts, and also becoming, as it were, an integral part of popular folklore. Even if we make allowance for the fringe of sentimentalism and of the superstitious magic characteristic of that age, we can say that this devotion reached its peak and, as it were, its golden age in the second half of the Middle Ages.

As a result of meditating on the life of Christ as portrayed in the gospels, and as a result of the development of Christological doctrine, a problem slowly arose that keenly interested the spiritual writers and mystics: the place of Christ's humanity in contemplation. Jean-Marie Déchanet contributed extensively to the research undertaken on this subject, and more specifically on the role of mediation that Christ's humanity plays in Christian contemplation. Going back to the sources that nurtured the mysticism of William of Saint-Thierry, he discovered the *eastern light* that had enlightened Origen, the friend of St. Bernard, and his main guide along the path of contemplation.

The Fathers of the Church seem not to have tackled the problem we are posing. Their exegesis—that of St. John, for example—remains cautious on this point, and Christological discussions perhaps polarized minds too exclusively. Whatever the case may be, the field of research is wide open. It is possible to follow the progress of the question beginning with the High Middle Ages. Multiple devotions to the humanity of

Christ, moreover, constituted a necessary stepping-stone and foundation for it, but many stopped there. However, William of Saint-Thierry was already speaking from experience, and so were others along with him. This experience became, if not more common, at least more frequently set forth by the principal representatives of the Carmelite school, for whom experience and teaching ordinarily went hand in hand. The reformers of Carmel asked the question and answered it clearly: Christ's humanity is the necessary means to contemplation. The scholastic theoreticians formulated a doctrine which, in its broad outlines, remains definitive.

Chapter I

The Fathers of the Church: The Formation of a Christian Sensitivity

by Irénée Noye, S.S.

A. *The First Three Centuries*

It is certainly difficult to speak of a "devotion" on the part of the Christians of the first centuries to the humanity of Jesus. The "Do not hold me" spoken to Mary Magdalene who had come to anoint Jesus' body (Jn 20:17) seems to have been their rule: now glorified, Christ was no longer to be regarded by them as a mere man. The New Testament writings, excepting the gospel accounts which are already remarkable for their sobriety, only briefly recall to mind "the days of His flesh" (Heb 5:7) and the reality of His human life "seen with our eyes . . . and touched with our hands (1 Jn 1:1). Many texts express a deep devotedness to the person of Christ, without, for all of that, eliciting homage or tender affection for His condition as a slave (Phil 2:7), or even the protracted gaze of the believer. The hymns incorporated into the Pauline epistles sing of the work and primacy of Jesus, but only passing mention is given to His manifestation in the flesh, a single phase in "the mystery of our religion" (1 Tm 3:16). The "Son of man," the only one of all the messianic titles that "Jesus applied to Himself,"[1] according to the synoptic Gospels, was used only a few

3

times in the New Testament and in primitive Christianity; it never led to a special consideration of the human aspects of the Messiah; it was pregnant with a technical and theological meaning[2] which drew attention to the redemptive work of the new Adam far more than to His humanity.

The prayer of the Christians of the first centuries also was directed "to Christ as to a God," according to the testimony Pliny the Younger gave of Him in his famous letter to Trajan.[3] This point greatly astonished the pagans who were sensitive to the fact that religious homage was directed to someone who had been crucified. The censures expressed in the second century by Lucian and by Celsus were still current at the beginning of the fourth century when Arnobius restated them so he could refute them: "You maintain that a man, born a human being, and one who suffered the penalty of crucifixion . . . was God, and you believe that he still exists and you worship him in your daily prayers."[4] Christians do actually adore "Christ as God"; but preoccupation with extolling His divinity results in not lingering over His human aspects. For example, the hymn that concludes *The Educator* of Clement of Alexandria sings of the "teacher of wisdom . . . the inexhaustible Word . . . Christ the King."[5] In this glorification of the pre-existing Word, we must undoubtedly see the reflection of the current of thought that will dominate theology from the third to the sixth century: "The Logos concept plays such an important role that all other titles are more or less suppressed."[6] Those writers who prefer to give Jesus the title of *Lord* thereby underscore His definitive glorification and His universal sovereignty.[7] The idea of the mediation of Christ in every prayer to the Father was so strongly stressed[8] that some wanted to forbid praying directly to Jesus Christ.[9]

Many texts express the communion of the martyrs with the Passion of Jesus; the attitudes and corporal sufferings of these witnesses are so many homages, often explicitated by the narrator, to the first "martyr."[10] Even when it is accompanied by an intense desire "to imitate the Passion of my God,"[11] this homage is directed much more to the living and life-giving Christ, "King and Saviour,"[12] than to His human existence.

Did the keen awareness which the first Christian generations had of the Saviour's glory entail a lesser esteem for His sojourn "in the flesh"? It is a fact, at least, that His humiliation in suffering, "a stumbling block to Jews, and folly to Gentiles" (1 Cor 1:23), remained disconcerting. The Apostolic Fathers rarely recall the Passion to mind except by way of the texts of the Old Testament (Is 52-53; Ps 21), as if they were taking refuge behind the authority of the prophets so that a truth too hard to bear might be accepted,[13] and all the more so in the polemic with the Jews.[14]

Inversely, the heresy of the Docetists led the Doctors of the Church to recall to mind the reality of Christ's earthly existence.[15] Nevertheless, the theology which began to be formulated beginning with St. Irenaeus on the union of the humanity with the Word did not yet include a "devotion" to Christ. Did it not even preserve some trace of a contempt of the flesh? In the creed that he quotes in *Against Heresies,*[16] Irenaeus affirms that "Jesus Christ, the Son of God . . . *tolerated* being begotten of the Virgin," echoed by the "non-horruisti virginis uterum" (you did not disdain the Virgin's womb) of the *Te Deum,* even if one agrees to adopt the variant "suscepisti hominem" (you accepted to become a man) which it tones down somewhat.[17]

It was, however, theological reflection which brought it about that more attention was given to the humanity which the Word did not disdain. The preoccupation of the Fathers of the third century was certainly not devotion; but even when they retain an especially intellectualistic view of the work of Christ considered as the revelation of God, their writings nonetheless do not remain cold speculations; their faith makes them aware of someone who was a living man, concretely inserted into the human race. Throughout the apologetic argumentations that bring out the genealogy of Mary's Son, Jesus' external comportment, His development, His fasting, His fatigue, His tears,[18] we sense a tone of gratitude coming through for "the well-beloved Jesus Christ, our Lord,[19] or an admiration for "the holy flesh woven in the Spirit," as Hippolytus says.[20] This becomes even more evident in the writings of Origen.

For Origen, knowledge of the man Jesus is only one step toward the knowledge of God; for humanity is a veil, a shadow. It is a sign that must be transcended.[21] Origen's philosophical formation, "so closely bound up with Middle Platonism," causes him to place much greater emphasis "on the eternal revelation of God than on the special event of the Incarnation."[22] But this need to go beyond the visible, to read the invisible through the visible, led him to scrutinize the visible attentively; and it is a paradox that the search for the meaning hidden in the Scriptures was a great help first of all to reading them well.

Origen also carefully commented on the gospel narratives; his method, which saw in every perceptible act a significance that escaped the senses, led him to explain Jesus' behavior and attitude.[23] In his homilies especially, "he pays particular attention to the gestures and ways of acting of those near Jesus"; he explains how people approach Him, how they receive Him, how they are acquainted with His home or are even allowed to rest on His chest.[24] Even if we must go beyond the "moralizing tone" of many of the texts relative to the imitation of the Word,[25] the faithful disciple is nonetheless invited to consider himself as participating in the episodes of Christ's life: "May you also find Him as you search for Him with Mary and Joseph";[26] regarding Simeon: "Behold, you are now standing in the temple of the Lord, that is, in His Church";[27] "Let Jesus wash our feet just as if we were His disciples."[28] In this way, Christ is very close to the Christian, not only in His risen life, as the faith of a Paul or of an Ignatius of Antioch could affirm His presence, but through the concrete episodes of His earthly life. When Origen speaks of Christ,

> we discern an accent of tenderness that is characteristic of him ... He praises those who contemplate Christ and who remain united to him "by a bond of tender affection." "My Jesus," he says, "my Lord, my Savior." This personal note became so much a habit with him that he ultimately injected it into his citations. There is something new in this, like a conquest of Christian piety.[29]

B. How the Doctors of the Church Speak of Jesus

The great epoch of Patristic literature (fourth and fifth centuries) did not so much retain Origen's views of spiritual ascent by means of contemplating Jesus the man, or his tender accents, as they did the method by which he introduced his readers to the realization of the Christian mysteries. This meth-

od, habitually followed from then on, was a commentary on the
gospels, in which attention to the human traits of Christ gives
rise to a discreet emotion. Didymus of Alexandria, Cyril of
Alexandria, Jerome, *et al.,* wrote explanations of the gospels.
The commentary was often preached first. John Chrysostom
delivered ninety-one homilies on Matthew's Gospel, and just
about the same number on St. John's. Augustine preached a
part of his *Homilies on the Gospel of John.*[30] Now the oratorical genre easily lends itself to more developed, even to more
realistic, recollections of the deeds of the Saviour. For instance,
commenting on Jesus at Jacob's well, John Chrysostom wrote in
a homily:

> He was seated; He was regaining His strength; He
> was enjoying the cool breeze near the fountain. It was
> noon. The evangelist tells us this by saying: "It was about
> the sixth hour," and He "sat down beside the well." What
> does that mean He "sat down"? Not on a seat, not on a
> cushion, but quite simply on the ground.[31]

Preaching is the necessary complement of liturgical celebrations and, even though these celebrations primarily aim at expressing the idea of salvation in Jesus Christ, they give them an
aspect of historical commemoration in which the humanity of
Christ, the instrument of this salvation, is honored; the faithful, participating in the liturgical feast, are also invited to take
part in a spiritual way in the gospel scenes:

> Like the tethered colt, let us bind ourselves indissolubly
> to Christ. If we seek salvation in the celebration of His
> feasts, He will raise us up with Lazarus from our dead
> works which have been performed without God (Heb
> 6:1) and we shall dine with Him at Bethany ... and we
> shall collect our thoughts together with the senses of our
> body by drawing them out of the captivity of oblivion,
> crying out and saying "Hosanna."[32]

The principal authors who have written or spoken of Jesus'
childhood are mentioned elsewhere;[33] an even greater number
of passages dealing with Christ's Passion could be added. One

might say that Christ's humanity is present everywhere in this
literature which never tires of contemplating and expressing its
faith in Christ Jesus. However, His humanity is never considered in itself because the authors had a keen awareness of
the unity of the mystery of Christ as well as its complexity, and
their purpose was different. Doctors and preachers had to in-
tervene in dogmatic, trinitarian, christological, and soteriological controversies. Likewise, when faced with the acts of the
Incarnate Word, they are careful to specify what is of man
in order the better to affirm what is of divinity. It is His
divinity that must be proved, defended, and honored against
Arianism and Nestorianism. The contemplation of the man
Jesus is in the service of this theological preoccupation. Our
attention is turned to Christ the new Adam, and consequently
to the relationships between the personal humanity of Jesus and
the universal humanity of men who are saved in Him. It follows, therefore, that for each author attention to the humanity
of Christ takes into account his Christology and his anthropology. It is easy to perceive these theological aims in St.
Ambrose's texts on the Passion.

Regarding Jesus' agony at Gethsemani, the Bishop of Milan,
who "nowhere else more admires his tenderness and majesty,"
not only analyzes the pedagogy of the Saviour ("How shall we
imitate you, Lord, unless we follow you as man, unless we believe that you are dead, having seen your wounds? How would
the disciples have believed that you are going to die if they
had not observed the anguish of a dying man?"), but even the
psychology of the God-Man as He faces death.[34] Yet, like
most of the Fathers, Ambrose remained dominated by theological problems: what pertains to Christ's body does not
affect His divinity.

> When we read of Jesus' arrest, beware lest we hear and
> believe the one who tells us that He is arrested as God,
> that He was arrested despite himself, arrested because He
> was powerless. True, He was arrested and bound . . . in
> the reality of His body; but woe to those who enchain
> the Word! He is enchained when all we see in Him is
> a man.[35]

Neither does Ambrose make a point of rendering adoration

to the humanity of Christ, because His passible body is no longer with us: "His corporal death does not need our attentions," he said, when speaking of the anointing at Bethany; it is His Church, the poor, who now require that we honor His body and His cross in them.[36]

The last point marks another direction of the thought of the Patristic period: the "body of Christ" is not only the physical body born of the Virgin, but is henceforth also His Church and the sacrament of His flesh given as food. Hence, we have these developments of St. Augustine, among many others:

> Let us always hear, or almost always hear, Christ's words in the psalms in such a way that we not only look at the head, the one and only mediator between God and men, the man Jesus Christ (1 Tm 2:5), He who by His divinity was in the beginning the Word, God from God, for the Word became flesh, and He dwelt among us (Jn 1:1.14), flesh of the race of Abraham, a descendant of David through the Virgin Mary; let us think not only of Him who is our head when we hear Christ speak; let us think of Christ, head and body, a sort of complete man.[37]
>
> Jesus Christ is one man with head and body, the Saviour of the body and the members of the body, two in one flesh, in one single voice, and in one passion; and when iniquity will have come to an end, two in one single repose. Christ's sufferings likewise are not in Christ alone.[38]

And in a commentary on the parable of the wicked rich man:

> The ulcers are the sufferings of the Lord in the infirmity of the flesh that He deigned to assume for us; and the dogs that lick them are the pagans whom the Jews considered sinners and impure, and who now throughout the entire world lick the wounds of the Lord in the sacraments of His body and blood with the greatest joy and piety.[39]

Solicitous for theological precision and fulfilling their duty to teach, the Fathers of the Church rarely gave a personal expression of piety to their christological or soteriological developments. The accent of affection toward Jesus Christ as man which often comes through in Origen's writings remains the exception. Not that these men were indifferent to the work of salvation, but their grateful love was directed more toward the risen Christ, even more often to the Father who handed over His Son. As long as Christology was not exactly defined, a cult of the humanity of Christ might be interpreted as a proof of the Nestorian position. Canon 9 of the second Council of Constantinople (553) anathematizes "anyone who advocated two adorations, one addressed to God the Word, the other to the man"; but at the same time, addressing itself to the Monophysites who "would do away with His flesh," it anathematizes "whoever does not adore in one and only one adoration the incarnate Word of God with His own flesh, according to the primitive tradition of the Church."

And yet, even in dogmatic formulations and precise distinctions, a sentiment of brotherhood with the God-made-man, a pride in sharing the human nature He assumed, discreetly comes to the fore:

> When Paul says: "God has exalted Him," he is speaking of His body. For it is not the Most High who is exalted but the flesh of the Most High, and it is to the flesh of the Most High that He gave a name above every other name. . . . It is not the Lord of glory who is glorified, but the flesh of the Lord of glory; it is His flesh that receives glory when it ascends to heaven with Him. . . . When did He converse with men (Bar 3:38), if not when like them He was born of a woman, when, like them, He was a little child, when, like them, He grew up with them, and ate with them.[40]

Some even go further, and their faith in the Incarnation is also expressed in a special veneration for the humanity of the Saviour, for example, Eustathius of Antioch (†337?).[41] The narratives that are constructed of the episodes of Christ's life stir up emotion and attachment to Christ as He was, as He is represented. For instance, when St. John Chrysostom (†407) speaks of Jesus' appearances to His Apostles, he says:

> Undoubtedly on hearing these things, your fervor has been

kindled and you say: Blessed are those who witnessed these scenes, and also those who will be with Him on the day of the general resurrection. Yes, let us do everything in our power so that we, too, may one day see this wonderful face. Merely listening, we are aflame and we would like to have lived in those times when He lived on earth, to have heard His voice and seen His face, to have been near him, touched Him, and waited on Him; what will it be, then, to see Him, no longer in His mortal body, no longer in His human actions, but surrounded by angels, we likewise, in a body freed from death, contemplating Him and savoring the happiness that defies all that can be said of it?[42]

An anthology of texts could be drawn up in which St. Augustine (†430) expresses his sentiments toward Christ in the flesh, especially toward the suffering Christ. Commenting on Ps 21 during the solemnity of the Passion, he cried out:

We celebrate the Passion of the Lord; it is the time to groan, to weep, to confess our sins and to implore. And who among us can shed tears worthy of so great a sorrow? Even if the fountain of tears (Jer 9:1) were in our eyes, it would not suffice.[43]

But such moments of emotion must not conceal the fact that the essential is elsewhere. The theologians of the Incarnation see in the humanity of Christ the instrument of salvation and therefore they do not stop there. Commenting on Ps 118: 27 ("Bind the festal procession with branches, up to the horn of the altar"), Augustine invites us to go beyond a human knowledge of the Lord: "I say to you clearly, brothers, all those who wish to understand the God-Word should not be satisfied with the flesh which the Word became for them in order to nourish them with milk; let them not be content with the feast day when the lamb was immolated; let them form a procession—the Lord lifting our minds—in order to attain even the inner divinity of Him who deigned to offer us His external humanity."[44]

It would seem that the Doctors of the Church who are most

concerned with showing the humanity of Christ as the way to union with God are the very ones who also sang its praises with the greatest fervor: Origen, then Augustine, and later St. Bernard. But is not the Gospel of St. John already the most speculative as well as the most affective?

C. The Beginnings of a Realistic Piety

The earliest theologians and preachers furnish us, therefore, with a doctrine of the humanity of Christ more than they do a devotion. In the course of the fourth century we perceive the first elements of a piety endeavoring to honor Jesus in His humanity.

1. The Evolution of Christian Art

It would seem that the first centuries knew of no portrait of Jesus; it even seems that a picture of Christ purported to be authentic would for a long time have smacked either of paganism, which it was advisable to avoid, or of Gnostic or syncretist circles. On the other hand, in addition to the symbols of the redemptive role of Jesus (the fish, the peacock, the lamb, etc.), the representations of a few gospel scenes from the third century have been preserved. They were retained not for their narrative value, but as significant of salvation (Jesus with Lazarus, the Samaritan woman, the paralytic, the calmed storm). Images of Christ alone depicted as the Good Shepherd, the philosopher or the teacher in the act of teaching, or with the features of Orpheus, illustrate the themes that were explained in the writings of the Fathers of the Church. These representations, therefore, always speak of Christ's role in regard to the baptized soul more than of seeing Jesus for Himself.

Beginning with the era of Constantine, iconography tended to become more narrative, more concrete: childhood scenes appear (the adoration of the shepherds and of the Magi); Christ is a young man in the midst of young Apostles (Rome, St. Domitilla). This historical, if not yet realistic trend, is temporarily eclipsed by the powerful movement that expresses both the triumph of Christianity over paganism and the victory of the faith of Nicea: the themes of Christian art undergo the influence of the scenes of the imperial court; everything there contributes to give Christ a royal, super-human aspect that will become more pronounced. By the end of the fourth century, Christ is represented seated on a throne or on a mountain, even above the sky, or else He reigns, as in the vision of the Apocalypse, surrounded by twenty-four elders or the four living creatures. The Theodosian era develops these traits and they will hold sway for a long time; the apses of the basilicas are adorned with monumental Christs in glory or on the cross (for the sixth century, at Rome, St. Lawrence-outside-the-Walls, Sts. Cosmas and Damian; at Ravenna, St. Vitalis; at Naples, St. John, etc.). Emphasis is upon the exaltation of the Son consubstantial with the Father, upon homage to Christ the king, upon the triumph of the cross which is often bedecked with jewels or gleaming with gold. The man Jesus has received "the name above every other name" (Phil 2:9). The movement grows stronger in the East in the last third of the sixth century when the representations of Christ are modelled after "acheiro-poietic" images: a half-length Christ with a strong face, a thick head of hair, a short, triangular beard and penetrating eyes. The miraculous origin that was conferred on these images brought them special honors: incensation, a triumphal chariot. The emblems with which they were adorned (scepter, the book of the Word of God, the verse "I am the light of the world") were proof enough that their purpose was to exalt the Word. The Orient was to venerate under the name of Pantocrator this superhuman Christ "who rules all things and contains all things."

Nevertheless, representations of the life cycle of Christ, sketched even before the triumph of Christianity, also find a place in the great era of ancient Christian art and inject a certain realism into it. If the scenes represented in the mosaics of St. Mary Major in Rome (around 430) or of St. Apollinaris at Ravenna (the beginning of the sixth century) are influenced by the majestic setting that shelters them, the illustration work of the gospel manuscripts, both in the East and in the West (Sinope, Rossano, Zagba in Mesopotamia, *Corpus Christi* of Cambridge—all of the sixth century), abandon all hieraticism and express the dramatic character of the scenes and personages . . . and even the personal, physical aspect of the actors of the gospel drama.

The two oldest pieces that remain of those which represent
Christ on the cross, the ivory casket preserved in the British
Museum in London and the panel of the old door of St.
Sabina in Rome, are believed to date from the fifth century.
In both cases, the almost nude Christ keeps His eyes open, and
there is no indication of suffering. These two pieces were surrounded by other scenes, the crucifixion being contemplated
only as one moment in the history of salvation. It is possible
that both of them are Syrian in origin; and the first representation that has been preserved of an emotion having to do
with the Passion comes from Syria with the work of a monk,
Rabbula, for the gospel book of Zagba in 586. The affliction of
the Virgin and of St. John at the foot of the cross, even when
the Crucified One is represented as living or even glorified, will
be a permanent theme and will take on greater importance in
the iconography of the tenth and eleventh centuries, a proof of
an evolution of sentiment regarding Jesus on the cross. It would
seem that there are no representations of Christ dead (eyes
closed, body prostrate with grief) before the ninth century
(the two gospel-books at the Pierpont-Morgan Library in New
York). Christian piety, therefore, gave the Saviour the features
of a simple humanity or condescended only very slowly to look
at Him in His humiliations.

2. The Veneration of the Cross

The veneration of the cross has already been treated in the
article *Croix*,[45] and another article has studied *Les Instruments
de la Passion*.[46] A. Frolow's recent thesis calls attention to
all the manifestations of this veneration between the second
half of the fourth century and the end of the Middle Ages; it
enumerates more than eleven hundred attestations. Thanks to
the relics of the true cross, whose authenticity was hardly
challenged, one had the feeling of attaining Jesus Himself, of
manifesting adoration and gratitude to Him, of honoring His
body given up for us and His blood shed for us. There was
therefore a particularized veneration of the instrument of salvation long before there was a veneration of the Saviour's humanity, of His holy Face,[47] or of His wounds, for example; but
this mediation of the cross was bound to draw attention to the
mediation of Christ's humanity. For example, it was in honor

of a fragment of the true cross, received in Poitiers in 569, that Venantius Fortunatus[48] composed hymns whose poetic form did not exclude realistic expressions. These hymns, adopted for the liturgy of Passiontime, helped to spread the affective tone with which the human history of Jesus was to be recalled to mind.

3. The Veneration of the Holy Places

From the third century on, the veneration of the Holy Places had for some privileged ones been the sign of an attachment to what we today call "the Christ of history." The subject will be treated at greater length in the article entitled *Pèlerinage*.[49] Here, as in preaching and liturgical developments, the peace of the Church in the fourth century was determinative, and the movement was checked only by the rule of Islam over Palestine. Pilgrims have left "itineraries" that ordinarily are quite restrained, yet still manifest a concern to find the exact places of Christ's life. The most revealing of these manifestations of ancient piety is the text of Egeria which dates from the end of the fourth century. The document sheds considerable light on the places of the liturgy and of the gospel narratives in the formation of Christian sentiment toward Jesus Christ.

At the conclusion of the Patristic period, St. John Damascene (†749) gave accurate expression to Christian faith and piety, both of which were concerned with warding off every doctrinal deviation and with rediscovering the Lord as He manifested himself to men:

> There is, therefore, only one Christ, who is perfect God and perfect man. We adore Him with the Father and the Spirit together with His immaculate body in one adoration, because for us His body is not unworthy of adoration. In fact, we adore it in the one and only person of the Word who became its person. We do not worship the creature, because we do not adore it as a mere body, but as being one with the divinity, because His two natures belong to the one person and the one subsistence of the Word of God. . . . I am not introducing a fourth person in the Trinity, but I do confess the person of the Word of God and of His flesh to be one.[50]

Every action of Christ, every miracle worked by Him is sublime, divine, and wonderful. But the most marvelous of all is His precious cross. . . . We are signed with His cross on the forehead; it sets us apart from the infidels. . . . It is a staff for the sick, a crook for the sheep . . . a plant of resurrection, and a tree of eternal life. This precious and venerable wood on which Christ offered Himself as a victim for us, is itself to be adored, because it has been sanctified by contact with His most holy body and blood. And so too are the nails, the lance, the garments, and His holy places, such as the manger, the cave, Golgotha, the tomb from which arose life and salvation, Sion, the citadel of the churches, and all those places of which the ancestor of God, David, could say: We will adore the place where his feet stood. . . . We also adore the precious and life-giving cross, whatever it was made of, for our veneration is not directed to the material it was made of (God forbid!) but to whom it represents, Christ.[51]

Chapter II

The Fathers of the Church: Contemplation of the Humanity of Christ

On the subject of "contemplation in the New Testament," we refer the reader to the article by J. Lebreton.[1] Bracketing this study, we will find in the same article on contemplation[2] a series of highly competent researched analyses on the theories of contemplative life among the ancient philosophers and the spiritual writers of the first centuries of the Church. We shall cite one or the other of these studies further on. We shall not repeat them. Their aim was to show how biblical and Christian faith culminates in a mystical experience where contemplation plays a preponderant role. This is particularly true of certain Fathers of the Church.

We propose to show in a more precise way the relationship between the theories of the Fathers on contemplative life and their faith in the Incarnation of the Word of God. The question is a decisive one and is often debated. Expressing themselves in the cultural framework of Hellenism, the three principal authors whom we have retained for this inquiry were to realize, according to their personal genius, a true conversion of the intellect in order to adjust their ideas on the higher life of the human spirit to the central affirmation of their faith in a God-made-man.

It would be a great help to have at hand monographs on

the Patristic commentary of the Sixth Beatitude: "Blessed are the pure in heart, for they shall see God" (Mt 5:8), or of certain verses of the Fourth Gospel, such as 4:14: "The water that I will give him will become in him a spring of water welling up to eternal life"; 6:63: "The words that I have spoken to you are spirit and life"; 10:9: "I am the door"; of 1 Jn 4:16: "God is love"; or of Gal 2:20: "It is no longer I who live, but Christ who lives in me." Citations such as these recur in the writings of all the ancient mystical theologians, from Ignatius of Antioch to Maximus the Confessor, for whom the Incarnation of the Word figures more explicitly as the source and pole of their contemplative life.

A. *Origen (c. 185-253)*
by Charles Kannengiesser, S.J.

What does the contemplative life represent for Origen?

At the highest stage of the ascent of souls toward God, contemplation characterizes the activity of the "perfect." One might be tempted to reduce the religious universe of the Alexandrian genius to a theological psychology. As a matter of fact, the spiritual structure of man, as understood by Origen, according to the distinction of the soul *(psyche)* and of the mind *(nous),* underlies all his other distinctions. This structure, innate to our being, involves us in "the way of the Lord" at two complementary levels, which are also two successive and necessary stages of spiritual progress, first, the *praxis,* and then the *theōria.* The *praxis* signifies the practice of asceticism, the acquisition of virtues, the labor of beginners, the yet uncertain improvement of those making progress. But it is the *theōria* or "contemplation" that interests us here, and this interested Origen himself more than anything else. It is "the knowledge and science of divine realities."[3] Its perfection resides in the *"theologia,"* in the strongest sense of the word, that is to say, in grasping the trinitarian mystery of God: "What other perfection of knowledge is there than to know the Father, the Son and the Holy Spirit?"[4] In order to reach this summit, the perfect benefit by the kindnesses of the divine Spirit who imparts true "gnosis" to them. The illuminating Spirit fixes the soul of these authentic spirituals, *"pneumatikoi,"* in "a knowledge of God, embracing the knowledge of things both human and divine and their causes";[5] "theology" comes to crown this knowledge. Origen's mysticism is oriented toward an intellectual contemplation of the mysteries of life, of the world, and of God. It remains the mysticism of a teacher, which does not prevent it from being a mysticism of love as well.

Does the humanity of Christ affect the "gnosis" of Origen?

The question is a practical one: "Why would the soul not grow in such a manner that, ceasing to be beset by carnal desires, it has perfect vision, perfect understanding of the reasons why the Word became incarnate and planned things the way He did?"[6] Origen asked this question in the fifteenth of the forty-two stations marking the interior "exodus" toward God which the second last of his homilies on Numbers so admirably describes. Now at this fifteenth station, the soul precisely attains the stage above "gnosis." The meaning of the Incarnation of the Logos seems, therefore, to affect rather closely the crossing of the threshold of "the theoretical life." A doubt would have been permitted concerning this. In fact, "those who know only Jesus Christ and Jesus Christ crucified and who, thinking that the Word made flesh is all there is to the Word, know Christ only according to the flesh; such is the mass of men who are considered to be believers."[7] We cannot mix the "perfect" with this multitude, for the whole doctrine on the Word in His human condition is only "milk" for those who are still "little children" in Christ.[8] "And so fortunately," Origen continues, "we hasten to move on to principles of a higher order."[9] In short, "the elementary teaching on Christ" needs to be transcended; St. Paul is the first to bear witness to this.[10] The cleavage between the "simple" and the "perfect" even takes place, it would seem, in a very special way regarding this teaching. "For those who have been brought into the faith only recently the Word of God has the *form of a slave,* so much so that they say: 'We have seen Him, and He had neither form nor beauty'; but for the perfect He comes in *the glory of His Father,* so that they say: 'We saw His glory as the only Son, full of grace and truth.' "[11] Christ's humanity interests both the simple and the perfect, but from different points of view. Why does Origen insist on this difference? How can his "perfect

ones" avoid the reproach of despising the faith of the "simple
ones"? Does their understanding of the Incarnation remain
evangelical?

A "gnosis" based on the Incarnation of the Logos

"Christ's body is not something for Himself apart from the
Church which is His body ... and God did not join them as
two (independent beings), but in one flesh, forbidding man to
separate the Church and God."[12] With that we have a basic
reason why the contemplative life of the Origenian "gnostics"
is based on the mystery of the incarnate Word; they are members of that Church where the presence of Christ is universally
actualized. They even constitute that Church by priority over
all the other categories of Christians. Their contemplation remains consistent with the teaching of the Church, is nurtured
on the mystery of the Church, and contributes to actualizing the
universal incarnation of the Word in the Church.

But for an even more profound reason contemplation, in the
mind of Origen, is based upon the humanity of Christ, as on
the cornerstone and the only foundation possible for spiritual
progress. We wish to speak of Origen's understanding of Scripture. On the one hand, Origen does not see how true "gnosis"
can come about and develop other than by contact with the
Bible. On the other hand, this Bible, the privileged place of all
initiation into the mysteries of divine revelation consummated
in Jesus Christ, seemed to Origen to be written entirely by God
in view of and on the model of the Incarnation of the Word.
Regarding the genealogy of Christ, the *Commentary on St.
Matthew* notes: "This prophecy, according to its proper nature,
is intangible and invisible; but once written and, as it were,
incarnated in the Book, it is seen and touched. Likewise, the
Word of God, having neither flesh nor body, being neither seen
nor written according to his Divinity, once incarnate, was seen
and written."[13] Word incarnate, Word written: the basis of the
entire value of revelation, attached to the Scriptures, must be
sought in the effective history of salvation, of which Christ's
humanity remains forever and for all the center.

Origen's decisive role, which makes his work normative even
down to our day, is to have associated the status of contemplation, the higher form of the knowledge of Christ and the life

of prayer, with this ecclesiological and hermeneutical structure. Origen explicated the principles on which the entire Oriental and Latin tradition rests in this matter. While his remarkable affinities with the philosophical culture of his time led him to a contemplation of myths and symbols, sublime projections by which man would know himself better and would find his true place in the universe, Origen worked out an authentically Christian gnosis, since, in the final analysis, it remains centered on that sequence of concrete and contingent events that revolve around the Incarnation of the Word.

If the Alexandrian teacher insisted so greatly on the difference between the "simple" and the "perfect," precisely regarding the meaning of this Incarnation, the reason was that he judged it vital for the economy of salvation to distinguish between those who adhered to a material reading, or to a "praxis," of the Scriptures, and those who are capable of transmitting the true science, the *theōria,* of these Scriptures. In fact, if the statements in Scripture incarnate the Word in their own way, whose perfect incarnation is achieved in Christ's humanity, the understanding of the Scriptures, in its turn, actualizes and universalizes this same mystery of the humanity of Christ in the "perfect." Their contemplation becomes, therefore, essentially an *imitation* of Christ, based on the Scriptures. And so they would not separate themselves either from the faith or from the virtues of the "simple," but only from their ignorance. Far from being a philosophical theory, their contemplation by preference focuses on the *spiritual senses* and, on that account, is modelled in all its endeavors on the most humble actions of the gospels.

The soul captured by the fragrance of the Word's ointments is moved to follow Him. What will it do when the Word of God takes possession of its hearing, its sight, its touch, and its taste, so that the eye, if it can see the glory of the Son of God, would desire to see nothing else, nor would the hearing desire to hear aught else but the Word of life and of salvation. And the one whose hands have handled the Word of life will nevermore handle anything material or perishable; nor will his palate tolerate any other taste once it has tasted the Word of life, His flesh and the Bread that comes down from heaven. Compared to this sweetness, all other flavors will seem bitter to him ... He who shall have merited to be with Christ will taste and see the

sweetness of the Lord. His delight will not be restricted to the
single sense of tasting, but all his senses will delight in the
Word of life. Wherefore we earnestly beg those who hear these
things to mortify their carnal senses. They must not take anything we have said as referring to bodily functions, but rather
employ the divine senses of the inner man to grasp these things,
as Solomon says: "You shall find the divine meaning."[14]

B. Gregory of Nyssa (c. 331-after 394)
by Charles Kannengiesser, S.J.

We will look in vain to Gregory of Nyssa for a contemplation of the humanity of Christ in the sense of the spiritual
masters of the Latin Middle Ages. Yet it has been said of
him: "There is no witness of so affectionate a love for Christ
in all the literature of the ancient Church as in the writing of
Gregory of Nyssa, nor of a keenness comparable to his in the
perception of the mystery of the divine indwelling and of the
intimate presence of Christ in our soul in all its religious
depths."[15] How is the relationship between the mystery of the
humanity of Christ and the contemplative life presented by the
greatest mystical theologian of the fourth century?

Contemplation, as Gregory understood it

The eminent specialist of Nyssian spirituality, Cardinal Daniélou, describes the highest forms of contemplation according to
Gregory under the meaningful title: "The mystique of darkness."[16] The experience of interior darkness, joined to an immediate awareness of God's presence in the soul, is put, in fact,
at the very center of ecstasy, which God can bestow on the contemplative soul in the course of its final ascent toward Him.
This very darkness also takes place at the source of the irrepres-
sible and endless movement that urges the soul to know and love
better the One who draws him to His infinity. But it is striking
to note the absence of any allusion to the Incarnation of the
Word in this study. One may guess why. Contemplation is a
transforming vision, envisioned by Gregory in a very clear-cut
eschatological perspective. The beatitude to which this vision
aspires is that of the original paradise, regained beyond all the
limitations imposed by matter, and consummated in a gift of
self that prolongs itself indefinitely even into divine plenitude.

But the last two chapters of his book on Platonism and mystical theology[17] are still too partial a notion of the contemplative life according to Gregory. Under the title of mystical experience Origenian themes as characteristic as that of "mirror of the soul" or that of the "spiritual senses" are analyzed. In the last chapter, on ecstatic love, allusions are not wanting, either in the citations of the *Commentary on the Song of Songs* or in the exegesis that the author proposes, both to the baptismal liturgy and to the Eucharistic and paschal celebrations. We therefore find ourselves in the framework of an ecclesiology and an anthropology to which the Alexandrian founder of this form of mystical theology had accustomed us.

For Gregory, man is basically fallen from his primeval dignity, where he lived on close friendly terms with his Creator. By becoming incarnate, Christ united us to Himself and restored to us the divine friendship we had at the beginning. Whereas man is by essence subject to change, Gregory especially underscores the idea that the humanity of Christ redirects the dynamism of our nature toward the divine, instead of maintaining it in the cycles of matter. If the practice of the virtues is necessary, we have been taught them by Christ. If growth in the knowledge of God presupposes an on-going resemblance between God and us, again it is Christ, and the incarnate Christ, who will obtain this resemblance for us, for in Him alone God becomes visible and therefore imitable.[18] It is, therefore, right to conclude with W. Völker that the Nyssian "gnosis" "transcends the sphere of ethical values alone and rests on a deep relationship with Christ," since for Gregory "all knowledge of God basically remains linked to Christ."[19] Can we pinpoint the sense of mystical experience if Gregory envisions it in this way in relationship to Christ?

The role of the humanity of Christ in the
contemplative life according to Gregory

Gregory distinguishes two levels of mystical experience. Christ is the one and only necessary basis of this experience at both levels, but in a different way.

a. The mediation of Christ incarnate

At the first level, where the experience of the "mirror of the

soul" takes place and where the divine illumination occurs in
the exercise of the spiritual senses, there is no contemplation of
the humanity of Christ, properly so called; but the soul leaps
toward the divine beyond, thanks to an inner tension of which
it knows that the incarnate Christ is the source and end.[20] According to A. Lieske, Gregory goes beyond Origen precisely
on this decisive point:

> Origen knew very well that our higher knowledge of
> God and our mystical union with Christ are proportionate
> to our effective participation in the mystery of the God-
> Man. [The author refers the reader to the *Commentary
> on the Song of Songs* I: "for each and every soul draws
> and appropriates the Word of God to itself according to
> the measure of its capacity and faith."] But Gregory was
> the first to clearly conceive this participation as a mode
> of mystical knowledge and therefore to further define its
> nature in the sense of an intuitive experience of God.[21]

b. Christ's humanity turns contemplation toward Christ, as God

At the second and highest level of mystical experience, where
reigns the darkness of the soul, fully confronted with the infinite
incomprehensibility of God, the role of Christ's humanity is
linked to the immediate perception of the presence of God in
the soul. If the soul unites itself to this presence as in a mystical marriage, it does so because it knows it is drawn toward
Him who, first of all, condescended to come down into it: "We
can be lifted up toward the Most High only if the Lord who
lifts up the humble has stooped down to what is below. That is
why the soul that rises toward the things that are above asks
the help of the Transcendent One and begs Him to descend
from His majesty in order to become accessible to those who
are below."[22] As with Origen, the contemplative lets himself
be gradually identified with Christ.[23] He experiences, through
the wound of divine Love,[24] the crucified and paschal unity between the Church and Christ, her Bridegroom.[25] And if its
model is Moses, it is still according to the gospel that Moses
was the first to discover the symbolism of the burning bush.[26]
The entire thread of Gregory's *Life of Moses* and of his *Commentary on the Song of Songs* is, so to speak, composed of

citations from the gospels or from St. Paul. Völker was not wrong in pointing out to what an extent Gregory's "content of ecstasy is determined by the historical revelation" of God.[27]

C. St. Augustine (†430)
by Paul Agaesse, S.J.

Faith in Christ is central to Augustine's theology; and the contemplation of Christ is at the heart of his spirituality. Adolph Harnack stressed this: "Christ was the point of orientation of Augustine's soul, even from his youth. Consequently, the developments which seem to be purely philosophical with him are very often influenced by the fact that he is thinking of Christ."[28]

Augustine's conversion was, in fact, magnetized by his search for Christ. Each stage through which he moved toward the truth was transcended because he had not yet found Him. He stopped in his quest only when he had reached God in Christ and through Christ. "While still a boy," he wrote, "I had heard of the eternal life promised us through the humility of the Lord our God who stooped to our pride."[29] When, after the confused years of adolescence, he was once again seized by the love of wisdom after reading the *Hortensius,* he could write: "The only thing that dimmed my great ardor was the fact that Christ's name was not in it. By your mercy, my youthful heart had tenderly drunk in with my mother's milk this name of my Savior, your Son; and there it remained in the depths of my heart; however literary, polished or true a book might be, without this name it could not completely win me."[30]

The desire to find Christ attracted Augustine to Manicheism and also made him abandon it.[31] For a while he was seduced by the maxims of the Academy, but he quickly refused to entrust himself "to philosophers who were ignorant of the health-giving name of Jesus."[32] His reading of the Neoplatonists dispelled his intellectual difficulties and solved the problem of evil for him, but he was still not satisfied. He had not yet fully encountered Christ: "I prated just as if I were learned, but had I not sought the way in Christ, our Savior, I was doomed not to know but to perish."[33] He knew where he was going, but he did not know the way; for he was not yet humble enough to embrace the humble Jesus as his God.[34] Only when he discovered the lessons of the Incarnation and the Redemption in Paul's Epistles did Augustine learn that he reached the end of his long search: "These things became deeply rooted in me when I read the least of your Apostles."[35] Therefore, throughout this conversion, two themes are intertwined: the desire to possess the absolute Good and the impossibility of attaining it without Christ: "I sought the way to obtain the strength that would enable me to enjoy you and I did not find it until I embraced the Mediator between God and man, the man Jesus Christ."[36]

We must not be surprised, therefore, that, once converted, Augustine gives the mediation of Christ first place; the outstanding conclusion of Book 10 of the *Confessions* is a proof of this.[37] During his search Augustine had been the victim of a twofold error. During the Manichean phase he could not resign himself into believing that Christ had come in the flesh which he considered evil;[38] during the Neoplatonic phase all he saw in Christ was a man of eminent wisdom, not the Son of God.[39] He found the answer to this twofold error in the dogma of the Incarnation, as the faith of the Church presented it to him: "True man, true God, the whole Christ is God and Man: this is the Catholic faith."[40] But its theological expression is most often immersed again in a Scripture text, particularly in the commentary of the prologue of St. John's Gospel: "When I read, 'The Word became flesh and dwelt among us,' by means of my intellect I see the true Son of God in the Word; in the flesh I recognize the true son of man, both reunited in the one person, God and man, by an unspeakable gift of grace."[41] Each of the affirmations of this profession of faith is often developed in Augustine's writings. Christ is the Word of God, like unto the Father in all things; it is as though uttering Himself the Father begets His Son who is equal to Him in all things.[42] Christ is also true man. He took a rational soul and a human body. "He united Himself to this body and to this soul without losing anything of His divinity; He became fully man. . . . If Christ slept, if He was nourished by food, if He assumed all the feelings common to mankind, He did so to convince man that He took on human nature; in assuming it He did not destroy it."[43] These two natures are joined together in the unity of the divine person,[44] and this humanity never existed outside the

Word: "From the moment He began to be man, from that moment He is also God."[45]

Nevertheless, although it is essential to the mediation of Christ that he be God, Augustine attributes the mediating role to the humanity of Christ: "In so far as He is man, He is a mediator. But in so far as He is the Word, He is not an intermediary, because He is equal with God, God along with God, and at the same time one God."[46] Consequently, we understand the place that Christ's humanity holds in Augustine's contemplation; and this accounts for the fact that he concentrated his prayer, his meditation, and his teaching on Jesus. Harnack looked upon this as an original characteristic of Augustinian doctrine. "We must note," he said, "that this contemplation of Christ was a new element, and that Augustine was the first to reintroduce it after Paul and Ignatius."[47] Surely this is an unjust statement with regard to the Greek Fathers, but it emphasizes the dogma central to the thought and life of Augustine. It is through Christ that he had access to the knowledge of the Triune God; it is Christ whom he finds at the center of history; Christ who is the source of the Church and of the grace communicated through the sacraments; and lastly, Christ who enables us to go from this transitory life to the future life.

This mediation of the humanity of Christ, that arouses his admiration and gratitude, is especially seen under two aspects: the authority of Christ enlightens our intellect in order to fix it in the truth, and His grace frees us of our sins and heals our will in order to fix it in good.

The Incarnation brings it about that the very one who acted for us in time makes Himself known as the Son of God and thereby reveals the Father to us. One phrase Augustine often commented on is the text in which Christ said that He is the way and the truth: as man He is the way; as Son of God He is the truth. "Christ . . . is our science, and the same Christ is also our wisdom. He is the one who plants in us the faith concerning temporal things, who reveals to us the truth concerning eternal things. It is through Him that we go to Him, making our way through science to wisdom, yet without separating ourselves from this one and the same Christ in whom are hidden all the treasures of wisdom and knowledge."[48] This text explains, at least in part, the relation of *auctoritas* and of *ratio*

in the understanding of faith: we must believe to understand
and humbly accept the teachings of the man Jesus in order to
have access to the knowledge of the mystery of God. Augustine was less attentive to the details of the gospel scenes than
the spiritual writers of the Middle Ages, even though he briefly
summarizes and enumerates the signs by which Christ shows us
that He assumed all the weaknesses of the human condition.[49]
But most often he gathers all the actions and words of Christ
together into one and discovers in them one unique and continu-
ous example of humility, which is the basic lesson of the Incarnation. Pride is sin. In coming to us and becoming like us,
Christ reveals to us that God is humble because God is love
and because humility is inseparable from love. This is all the
more true since this love is gratuitous.[50]

On the other hand, Christ is the one who by His sacrifice
frees us from our sins, wins over our heart, and reconciles us
with God through the sacrifice of the cross. He is the one and
only Saviour.[51] Augustine could remember the time when, already enlightened by the light of truth, he remained a slave to
his passions. But the witness of Scripture became a living experience for him:

> I am indeed right in basing my strong hope in Him,
> that you will heal all my weaknesses through Him who
> sits at your right hand and intercedes for us with you:
> otherwise *I would despair.* These weaknesses are so many
> and so strong . . . But your remedy is even mightier. We
> might have thought that your Word was too far removed
> from any union with man and thus despair of ourselves,
> except for the fact that He did become flesh and dwell
> among us.[52]

The insistence on the redemptive act is such that Augustine even went so far as to say that Christ took a body to die
for us: "He was God and He came in the flesh in order to die
for us."[53]

The result of this marvelous exchange is that, because the
Son of God became man, man can become God:

> And so the Immortal One could die, and in that way
> willed to give life to mortals; next, He was to share His

life with those whose life He had first shared. For we
ourselves do not have the wherewith to live and He did
not have the wherewith to die. And so, in a mutual sharing, He made a wonderful exchange with us: that by
which He died belonged to us; that by which we are able
to live belongs to Him.[54]

As J. M. LeBlond points out, there is a certain tension in
Augustine between a Platonic theocentric mysticism and a
christocentric mysticism. Nevertheless, there seems to be no
opposition or contradiction between the two. Augustine's hope
and aspiration were always turned toward the vision of God.[55]
But, on the one hand, this knowledge of God can be given here
on earth only by faith in Jesus Christ; on the other hand, even
in the next life, when faith will have given way to vision, it is
again in Jesus Christ that the just will know the Father. "Let us
beware of thinking that Christ will hand over the kingdom to
God the Father by dispossessing himself of it . . . No, the man
Jesus Christ will lead all the just, in whom the Mediator of God
and of all men already reigns by their life of faith, to the contemplation which the Apostle calls the face to face vision."[56] It
is in this sense that J. M. LeBlond concludes: "Yet there is no
doubt that Augustinian mysticism is a mysticism of Christ . . .
Christ and the grace he confers have definitely transformed his
[Augustine's] thought as well as his heart, and his every effort
in the contemplation of the world, of men, and of history will
henceforth be directed to recognizing the *sacramentum Christi*
in them."[57]

Chapter III

The Medieval Masters

by Jacques Hourlier, O.S.B.

For those acquainted with medieval spirituality, one idea seems obvious and basic: Christ's humanity holds an important place in contemplation, in fact a central place for many authors. The subject, however, has hardly attracted the attention of historians, perhaps because they have been detained in their analyses by numerous works that are given over to the study of devotion and piety. For lack of a comprehensive account, it would be helpful if we could consult some monographs. But there are precious few of them, except for some preliminary studies relative especially to St. Bernard. Since this is the case, we shall divide our exposé into two parts: one dealing with the problematic, and the second with history.

A. The Problematic

The spiritual itinerary demands a grace merited by the redemptive Incarnation of the Word. Even though authors, such as William of Saint-Thierry, emphasize the role of the Holy Spirit in the work of sanctification and in our adhesion to God whose presence is felt in the soul, they do give a large place to the Incarnate Word. They envision His humanity from different perspectives, sometimes paying particular attention to the person of Christ, at other times to the actions of His life, and again to what they consider prolongations of His being.

1. The Person and Life of Christ

They never separate the divine nature from the human nature in the person of Jesus, even though they make a clear-cut distinction between the two. This presents a difficulty when we analyze their ideas on contemplation, unless we envision the union of the two natures as the kernel of their teaching, a point that clearly emerges even from a simple reading of their writings. St. Odile's sermons offer a rather clear example of this.

To the extent that they linger over Jesus' humanity, these authors do not, as a rule, distinguish between the soul and the body, or, to put it more precisely, they do not closely examine the psychology of Jesus. They more readily speak of the man like unto us, which the Incarnate Word is. On the other hand, they sometimes devote themselves to a more detailed treatment of Christ's body or of a particular part of His body. The wound in the side leads certain writers to speak of Christ's heart; through it they find access to the fullness of love.

Jesus' life, with its stages of birth, Passion, and Resurrection, reveals to the contemplative the infinite love of God for men. To meditate on His life can only lead one along the paths of contemplation. The difficulty here for the historian is to know whether he can recognize a distinction between the person of Christ and the fact of the Incarnation, for many authors seem constantly to change from the man Jesus to the Incarnate Word and vice versa, or even to soar to the eternal Word without saying that they are changing levels. This very comprehensive view of the mystery of Jesus indeed shows that it always leads toward more or less explicit contemplative perspectives. Now all these authors recommend meditation on the life of Christ, and more particularly on His Passion. This advice is a constant, common theme of medieval spirituality. Those writers who make such meditation a privileged exercise for beginners, for example, William of Saint-Thierry, Bernard of Clairvaux, and pseudo-Bonaventure, encourage these beginners not to abandon it later on; these very men can, moreover, set themselves up as models in this regard.[1] Does not eternal beatitude consist in contemplating Christ in His glory, adorned with the stigmata of His Passion?

The liturgy offers a privileged means of re-living the mys-

teries of Christ, thereby of uniting oneself with Him, of entering
into heaven with Him, and of seeing God. The sermons that
comment on the liturgical cycle provide one of our main sources
on this subject. We would like to be in a better position to
know what contemplative repercussions the orations and doxol-
ogies were able to awaken in souls; William of Saint-Thierry
took it upon himself to note how the conclusion of the orations
makes us go through our Lord to attain the Father.[2] The texts
of the Divine Office add their contribution. Without going into
detail, we shall limit ourselves to pointing out certain feasts:
Christmas, which sees the Saviour, God-with-us, the King of
Heaven in the Child; the Ascension, which especially in its
hymns and their melodies has an ecstatic quality about it; the
Transfiguration, a more recent feast, which gives greater emphasis to this contemplative orientation; *Corpus Christi,* when
the theme of the Real Presence leads to union.

One of the best authors who both lived and explained the
meaning of the liturgy, Rupert of Deutz, shows the link that
binds the liturgy on the one hand to the life of Christ, and on
the other hand to contemplation. The divine services

> contain the sacraments of heavenly secrets . . . they were
> instituted in honor of our Lord Jesus Christ by those men
> who had the sublime understanding of the sacraments of
> His Incarnation, of His birth, His Passion, His resur-
> rection and His ascension. . . . Those who attend the
> mysteries of the Church with faith and piety, without
> knowing the reasons for them, do not do so without
> fruit. . . . The secret, which can be understood by only
> the few, can be lived *(agi)* by all.[3]

2. *The Prolongations of the Humanity of Christ*

Medieval thought does not limit the humanity of Christ to
the person and life of Jesus: Christ's humanity is readily
granted all the dimensions that it attains in the divine plan and
associated with all that can have a relationship to it. In this
last orientation, we must give attention to the idea of making
pilgrimages to the Holy Land, joining to it the veneration of
the saints of the gospel. Some consideration must also be given
to the veneration of the relics of the Passion, relics either

properly so-called or figuratively speaking, especially of the holy cross. We shall not forget that architecture multiplied relics of the holy places, the holy sepulchers, for example, and the altars commemorating Christ's mysteries. Painting and sculpture bring out in greater detail the scenes of Jesus' life and center attention on the crucifix. Better than a simple devotion, before it on a historical plane, we find in the cross a means of meditation that easily issues into contemplation. The cross, crested with the paschal lamb, shored up by the four gospel symbols, then surmounted by two angels, expresses a theology that goes beyond the level of sentiment.

Besides these privileged witnesses, all creation bears a relationship with Christ. The Middle Ages looked upon creation as a manifestation of His goodness, if not as an expression of Himself, that was recognizable in human creatures and in angels. By this means, it arrived at the knowledge and the love of the Creator, an idea common to all times, but which it lived intensely by insisting on the reference to the Incarnation. Creatures, the lovable things of God, form the first panel of a triptych which leads through Christ to the divine essence.

The Middle Ages also saw the prolongation of Christ in Sacred Scripture and, perhaps more directly, in the sacraments. On this point we have to go back to the lessons which medieval exegesis gives us, with its predilection for edifying reading. It was almost entirely allegorical in style before the Victorines came along to insist on the literal meaning. The simplicity of the letter certainly offers helpful instruction for everyone, but we must go beyond it to appreciate the inner sense. Beyond the historical, allegorical, and moral senses, the anagogical leads to contemplation where, by divine love, the soul finds itself in some way united to the Divinity. This is the spirit in which the Middle Ages read and commented on all the Scriptures, including the gospels, and by which it knew how to find the person of Christ in all the sacred books.

The sacraments, and here we do not mean the hidden mysteries in the Scriptures or the liturgy, but the means of sanctification, the authentic instruments of grace, were considered both very efficacious means of union with the person of Christ and of contemplation of the Divinity. Rupert of Deutz and Gertrude of Helfta are excellent examples of this.

Another "sacrament," the Church, the spiritual body of
Christ, leads us along the road of contemplation, especially
when we envision her under her title of spouse of Christ. Here
we should recall to mind many of the commentaries on *The
Song of Songs*. In this perspective, the Virgin plays a role
which the sermons on the Annunciation, for example, underscore. And lastly men, as creatures and brothers of Christ, also
have a useful but less studied role than that of our Lady, a
role set forth, for example, when presenting the first steps of
love for God.

3. Contemplation

The humanity of Christ leads to contemplation by two ways.
It is taken either as the term of contemplation and union, or is
used as a means to attain in succession the eternal Word, the
other divine persons, God in His Trinity or in His unity. Faith
always intervenes to raise the soul up from the man Jesus to
the God hidden in Him. It carries out a primary work of
knowledge which the mystical life further extends. But it is
difficult to see at just what moment there is true contemplation,
and this makes the interpretation of many texts difficult.

If we want to lay down criteria that would enable us to
recognize the passage from ordinary knowledge to contemplation, we could summarize medieval thought relative to contemplation by saying that it presupposes that man is a friend
of God, therefore redeemed from sin and moved by grace. This
friendship enables him to look at God with love and thereby
obtain knowledge of Him, and to possess Him in a pleasing
way, while at the same time being possessed by Him. In the
union of two beings so far apart as the Creator and the creature, a mutual knowledge goes hand in hand with a love that
leads the human intellect into a progressive transcendence, a
mystical knowledge.

This mystical knowledge will be presented, especially in the
twelfth century, as the term of a series of operations beginning
with reading, above all with the reading of Scripture; but if a
distinction is made between contemplation and consideration,
meditation and prayer, one does not insist on the differences in
such a way as to exclude every form of contemplation from the
preliminary stages. Similarly, "theoretical" life is not separated

from "practical" life to the point that one would exclude the other; and likewise, man's states (animal, rational, spiritual), although indicating a progress, are rather considered as concomitant dispositions. In these conditions it is often difficult to separate simple devotion from true contemplation. To distinguish them in too absolute a fashion could be an anachronism, for it is rather the historian who sets up the frontier between them. He bases this on valid ideas, but it is not always so clearcut in the texts; it was less so in the minds of those for whom affection *(affectus)*, sentiment itself, already gave a certain vision of God. It makes no difference whether we reread many *Meditations*, so many *Revelations*, whether we think of the formula "love itself is knowledge" *(amor ipse notitia est)*, or whether we place such knowledge at the lowest echelon of the degrees of love; the distinction between contemplation and devotion will be legitimate only if evident proofs show that devotion cannot turn into contemplation; and even then the distinction will remain purely objective, hardly allowing us to divine the secret thoughts of men.

It would even be more ticklish to separate contemplation from union with God through Christ. Many medieval writings that speak only of union are to be classified as dealing with the contemplative life, especially before the thirteenth century. Many authors declare that meditation and prayer are indistinguishable; they go from devotion to contemplation quite natually by means of affection and illumination. They speak of the journey of the soul toward God, of a living encounter, of a fusion. Do they, for all of this, think of excluding vision, or, on the contrary, are the two similar? This is the whole problem of the distinction between knowledge and love, of the relationship between contemplation and union. It is a difficult problem if we expect to resolve it in itself; it is of lesser importance if we are willing to admit, in conformity with reality, that for the man of the Middle Ages these two aspects of the mystical life pervade each other. In fact, both are often developed by the same author and sometimes in the same passage of his writings.

To recall these data relative to medieval thought is to show that we must not build partitions when we interpret explanations that are somewhat systematic, especially when we try to probe deeply into the psychology of the authors of the Middle Ages, using as our sources witnesses that are in no way scholarly.

B. History

Centered on the twelfth century, the time most beneficial to our purposes, our historical essay is arranged quite naturally according to three periods of the Middle Ages: the High Middle Ages, the twelfth century, and the thirteenth century. The fourteenth and fifteenth centuries will be treated in the next chapter.

1. The High Middle Ages

St. Gregory the Great (†604) opens and dominates the Middle Ages. It would be interesting to determine precisely what this period and the centuries that followed retained of the teaching of this mystical doctor, and how it combined his interests with that of other minds, and first of all with St. Augustine. Such an investigation would call for a thorough study of such manuscripts as, for example, the *Codices Latini Antiquiores,* which were compiled prior to the ninth century, or of the quotations in the *Vitae* which were written during the High Middle Ages. Let us limit ourselves to two fairly contemporary witnesses, one emanating from a literary milieu, the other from an often less developed milieu; both enjoyed a long success.

Bede (†736) is an excellent model of the contemplative life in the cloister. Many pages of his writings show with what devotion he meditated on the life of Jesus and the mystery of Mary; and yet, he invites those who can to rise to a higher understanding of Scripture by way of allegory. He follows in the footsteps of another master of medieval spirituality, John Cassian, for whom the object of contemplation varies according to the degree of purity of those who pray: for some, Jesus in His humanity, for others, Jesus in His glory. The first devote themselves to works of the ascetical life, and Jesus shows Himself to them, but not with the same brilliance of glory as to the second, who follow Him on the mountain, imitating His own example when he withdrew to pray in solitude. Ambrose Autpert (†784) threw light on this way of thinking when he said that Christ is par excellence the object of contemplation and explained, for example, that we must contemplate the

Divinity under the appearances of the Child at the Purification.[4]
The common lesson is and will be during the entire Middle
Ages that one begins with the humanity of Christ's flesh to
reach the glorified body of the Risen One in the depths of the
Trinity.

The Irish have left us a form of prayer that found many ad-
herents, the "breastplates" *(loricae),* the beginnings of our litanies. While saying them, one meditated piously on God, mul-
tiplying invocations to the Trinity, to the mysteries of the life of
Jesus, and to the various parts of His body. Among the many
invocations, Christ is called the image of the Father, Divinity,
faithful light of love, and so forth; and one prayed for the
"theoretical" as well as for the active life.[5]

In the cloisters and in the milieu molded by them, Christians
meditated on Christ, both to imitate Him and in order to
achieve success in contemplation. The christocentric nature
of the Benedictine Rule has often been pointed out, but we
must not forget that, guided by the gospel, the monk reached
those summits of doctrine and virtue where one could recognize
a high contemplative ideal, in imitation of St. Benedict, such
as St. Gregory depicts in his *Dialogues.*

An abundant Carolingian literature continued and amplified
these aspects. Only one person contributed somewhat new
elements, but his success began only three centuries later:
John Scotus Erigena (ninth century). He thoroughly revised a
previous translation of the works of Pseudo-Dionysius, which is
of minor interest to our subject. But in his own work on the nature of man *(De Divisione Naturae),* his central ideas is essential
for us: God descends toward man through the Incarnation;
after His redemptive death, Christ the Mediator leads man to
God; through love and contemplation everything is found
united to God and in order, and Christ Himself has furnished
both the example and the means.

One century earlier, Paul the Deacon (†c.799) had defined
the common doctrine when he spoke of the gift of tears that the
monk obtained successively by lamenting his sins and invoking
the saints, by uniting himself to the mysteries of the Incarnation of the Son of God, and by acknowledging the Trinity; and,
proposing a night prayer, he said in regard to the second means:
"Lord Jesus Christ, I believe that you were announced by the

angel to the Virgin Mary . . . were born . . . shown to the shepherds . . . circumcised on the eighth day . . . adored by the Magi,
baptized . . . betrayed by Judas . . . and rose . . ."[6]   Compare
with this text, books 5 and 6 of the *Occupatio,* of Odo of Cluny
(†942), where he speaks of the Incarnation, then of the Eucharist and of the triumph of Christ. The preceding books
treat of the fall of the angels and of man, then of the prototypes
of the Old Testament, whereas the last book foretells the
Antichrist and the end of the world. This historical perspective is likewise a constant of medieval thought. It situates the
person and life of Christ in the unfolding of time, whose final
stage is for every man as for the human race consummation in
God, and therefore the beatific vision, which here below is
anticipated through contemplation.

2. The Twelfth Century

Despite the political and social upheavals resulting from the
destructive raids of the ninth and tenth centuries, spirituality
did not lose any of the heritage it had received. In particular
it continued its penchant for the history of the Word-made-
flesh and for His person. It was enriched with new elements.
On contact with evils, emotional response became more refined
and found means of expression. The contribution of Carolingian
France was enhanced by what the monks of northern Italy,
who spread to Burgundy and Normandy, gave it between the
tenth and twelfth centuries. These monks also ushered in an
attempt at philosophical reflection, which was destined to yield
a great harvest. Three orientations characterized this spirituality; they are not trends, still less schools, but aspects that were
easily combined. They can be characterized by three words:
history, sentiment, and reasoning.

Interest in "history," even if joined to allegorical interpretation, was readily accompanied by artistic imagination. It led
to those Roman tympana, the most perfect example of which
is at Moissac. The Cluniac Order contributed greatly to the
elaboration of the theme and to its spread. This contemplation of Christ in His glory represents the term of a meditation on Jesus' life. Its sculptural expression, which appeared
slightly later, betrays an exquisite sensitivity (e.g., the engaged
piers of Moissac, the portals of Charity). Delicacy of sentiment

does not exclude theological doctrine. To be convinced of this, it would suffice to know how much authors like St. Odilo, for example, stress the union of the two natures.[7] The historian of art is familiar with the long durations of these iconographic themes. The 'beautiful God' on the pier of Gothic cathedrals always offers the vision of the God-Man to the attention of anyone who enters the temple of the Lord, but this art of the thirteenth century is less conducive to the true contemplation of the divine majesty because other influences have encumbered it with encyclopedic and moral preoccupations.

To appreciate this "historical" orientation of spirituality at its correct value, we must envision it as it really was: less a glance at the past than a present participation in it, not by experiencing sentiments, but by living with Christ. We must insist on the actuality of the Incarnation for each man here and now, on the continuity of divinization. The importance of the liturgy and especially of the mystery of the Eucharist flows from this. Rupert of Deutz (†1129) and Peter of Celle provide us with many examples.

The development of spiritual sensitivity does not mean sentimental affection, as we often find it in milieux where the intense ascetical effort was directed toward forms of eremitical life. Many recluses, St. Peter Damian (†1072), for example, or the Carthusian Guigo II (†1193),[8] stress the Saviour's sufferings and are content with nothing but the cross, "leaving to others the majesty of the Divinity." To do this is perhaps to put limitations on the contemplative riches offered by Christ's humanity.

Ordinarily the authors exploited more fully the resources which the humanity of the Word offered them. If John of Fécamp (†1078) preferred to all else the contemplation of Christ's Divinity, he also knew how to linger over the mysteries of Jesus' life; reading led him to devotion, pure prayer, and contemplation. As for St. Anselm (†1109), we have only to compare his *Prayers and Meditations* with his *Cur Deus Homo* and his *Proslogion* to appreciate the depth of his thought when confronted with the God-Man, even beyond his effort at reasoning.[9]

The eventual bond between devotion and contemplation is less easy to discern among the Victorines, who are too intellectualistic, too influenced by the Dionysian idea of renunciation of every representation when claiming the attainment of union with God. Certainly, the fourth degree of charity for Richard consists in this, namely, that the soul is configured to the humility of Christ; but in this speculative and excessively methodical mysticism, Christ's humanity remains in the background. We notice this even when the Victorines approach the lyric genre, for example, in the sequences of Adam of Saint-Victor.

The exact opposite happens in the milieux where sentiment and reason are closely joined together, whether they apply their psychological analyses to the structure of the soul or to its emotional response. Two names characterize these milieux: William of Saint-Thierry (†1148) and St. Bernard (†1153).

For William of Saint-Thierry, contemplation consists in a participation in the life of the divine Persons when they dwell in the soul. Although the Holy Spirit plays a determining role in it because He is the love who takes possession of man, the incarnate Word holds an important place in William's spirituality. As Redeemer, He restores the image of divine resemblance in the soul; furthermore, He is the One who sends this Spirit to men, the Spirit who likewise proceeds from the Father and the Son. He is the model. Specially recommended to novices, to the animal man, Christ in His human form, in the recollection of His earthly life and of His Passion, makes possible access to God.[10] Moreover, even in His human manifestations, Christ enables man to attain the power of His divine operation.[11] The spiritual man has no experience of Jesus living according to the flesh among men; he finds Him glorified, but clothed with human flesh in heaven whence His blood always flows for the redemption of believers.[12] Christ is the door leading to the Father; His person, His cross, His Eucharist, and His heart obtain for man the vision of God face to face. In fact, by His Incarnation, His Passion and His death, He reveals the Father's love for men and His own love both for the Father and for mankind.[13] He manifests Himself to men and shows the Father to them. As mediator, He enables us to pray, to adore, and to unite ourselves to God. The formula "through the Son in the Spirit" was dear to William. In giving the Spirit, Christ Himself was able to fulfill His request to the Father: "That they may be one, even as we are one" (Jn 17:11).[14]

William of Saint-Thierry thought in terms of being. St. Bernard places himself more on the plane of action; despite points which are common to both, St. Bernard's lesson is different. Basically, we can make the distinction between flesh and spirit. In becoming incarnate, the Word addresses Himself to both, and unites Himself to both, because He, too, is spirit and flesh. In studying man's union with Christ, Bernard benefits from an ardent sensitivity, with the result that the mystery of Jesus becomes alive in all its manifestations and prolongations, in our Lady evidently, but also in all spiritual and material creatures.[15] He gladly returns to the psychological role that Christ exercises from the fact that He knew human misery. He bestirs the soul; He paves the way for recollection, and therefore for contemplation. He gives man the experience of being one with Him, and therefore of imitating Him and of conforming himself to Him. He makes known God, His benevolence, and His goodness. He makes Him loved.[16] His person and His life convert hearts and illumine minds. Since they are the model of humility and especially of love,[17] these two virtues inform man's love for God.[18] Christ's humanity, however, directly interests only the first degrees of love, for it is a sacrament that, while giving access to the Divinity, hides it. We must rejoin Christ where He is now, attain and ascend to the eternal Word, and unite ourselves to Christ, the Bridegroom, by going beyond His shadow, that is, His flesh.

Yet for all of this, Bernard does not abandon Christ's humanity, for he never separates the two natures of Jesus from each other, or the different acts of His earthly life from His state of heavenly glory. If, at a certain degree of contemplation, he asks us to give up every material image, it is always the Word who was born of Mary and died on the cross that the soul attains, even beyond any experience of the senses.[19]

By way of summing up Bernard's doctrine, we might quote this sentence: "Contemplation results from the condescension of the Word of God to human nature through grace and the exaltation of human nature to this very Word through divine love."[20] And to remind ourselves that the other Cistercian writers, each with his own nuances, share a similar doctrine, we might take an example from Aelred of Rievaulx (†1167), a man devoted to the crucified Savior as much as he was to the twelve-year-old Child. For him the flesh of our Lord is the means whereby one makes the transition from concupiscence to charity. The soul can then escape the mask of the flesh and enter into the sanctuary where Christ becomes spirit, and in that way be absorbed in unspeakable light.[21]

3. The Thirteenth Century

The three centuries that follow the death of St. Bernard and of his immediate disciples are commonly thought of as a period in which doctrine becomes more and more clearly separated from devotion. Devotion considered the humanity of Christ; doctrine constructed the theory of contemplation and of union with God. This summary view calls for further clarification. The following chapter will attempt to show the real devotional and doctrinal continuity of the fourteenth and fifteenth centuries. We limit ourselves here to a few remarks regarding the thirteenth century.

The evolution of mentalities and the changes of emotional response do not do away with the previous orientations. At the end of the thirteenth century, the monastery of Helfta provides us with an example which is all the more significant in that it was not closed to new influences. The cloistered nuns, and first of all, St. Gertrude (†1302), lived the life of Christ according to the most traditional and most authentic liturgical piety. Their familiarity with the person of Christ flowed from a solid theological doctrine. Their entire mystical life led them to union with the Blessed Trinity through the intellect as much as through the heart.[22]

If we study the masters of theology, the Dominicans especially, the cleavage mentioned above becomes apparent as we read their writings. But were they aware of it? Such was the case with St. Albert the Great (†1280). Devout in his spiritual writings, he made no attempt in them at giving a doctrine. He reserved this for his scientific work. The same must be said of St. Thomas Aquinas (†1274), whose burning love for Christ is undeniable, whose balance between devotion and intellect, and intellectuality and piety, is acknowledged. However restrained he is in his theological statements, on occasion he affirms his conviction: Christ's humanity is supremely capable of bringing about "devotion," although the proper object of devotion is the Divinity, and devotion is the source of knowledge in which contemplation resides.[23]

St. Francis of Assisi (†1226)[24] bears witness to a very traditional spirituality, ending in an adoration of the Trinity, through Christ and in Christ. What was personal about him was the note of sincerity, of the absolute, which he put in the carrying out of evangelical perfection, otherwise called the imitation of Christ. The great Franciscan theologian, St. Bonaventure (†1274), also stresses love and imitation of Jesus crucified. The *Itinerarium Mentis ad Deum* proposes an habitual search for God in the traces He left of His presence and operation, for Christ is both "the book of eternal wisdom, the source of all knowledge, the teacher and principal doctor, the moral ideal to be imitated, and the norm of all morality."[25] Remembrance of the Passion and cross plays an essential role in the purgative way. The imitation of Christ holds a large place in the illuminative way. And in the unitive way, "inspection" or contemplation of Christ and of the Trinity leads to the "introduction" or mystical transition into God. "There are no stages where the incarnate Word does not loom as the beginning, the model and the end. The cross becomes the tree of life and the sum of divine illuminations; the crucified Christ constitutes the one and only point of transition toward ecstasy and the highest contemplation of the Trinity. Lastly, it is in communion with the body of Christ that the taste for mystical experience develops and where most often the Lord reveals Himself to contemplative souls."[26] St. Anthony of Padua, affectionately devout to Jesus both as child and crucified, assigned a twofold purpose to contemplation: God, enjoyed and experienced in the soul; and the humanity of Christ, joined to the Church triumphant.[27]

For the Carthusian Guigo de Ponte (†1297) speculative contemplation and anagogical contemplation likewise lead to union with God. In the first, Jesus heals, and therefore purifies. He is the one and only way to union, through meditation on His life and Passion. Grace gradually causes us to go from the humanity to the Divinity, from speculation to anagogy which attains the divine majesty.[28]

Chapter IV

The Golden Age of Medieval Devotion: The Fourteenth and Fifteenth Centuries

by André Rayez, S.J.

It is not our intention in the least to take up the theme of the devotion and contemplation of the humanity of Christ at the end of the Middle Ages in all its ramifications. We would simply like to speak of the importance of this devotion and of its forms, to recall to mind its traditional sources, and to show that devotion ordinarily led to contemplation. In these respects, the cult rendered to the humanity of Christ reveals itself to be an enrichment of the Church's piety and of her spiritual experience. Based on accepted dogmatic foundations and presented in comprehensible language, it preserves the faith of the faithful, strengthens it, and guarantees its renewal.

A. Climate and Mentalities

Christ's humanity and, secondarily, the humanity of the Blessed Virgin form the center of medieval devotions. Christ, God and man, has always been the main object of the cult of the faithful, of monks, and of the secular clergy. Nevertheless, the manifestations of this cult have evolved a great deal with time and mentalities. We have already spoken of "the birth of Christian sensitivity" in regard to the humanity of Christ.[1] It would seem that with the milieu of Bernard, a threshold was reached and then crossed. Christ's humanity moved the heart of the medieval Christian more and more; the cult, literature, and the arts made a special point of expressing sentiments and faith with a growing realism, which gives the impression of exploding or of flowering in the fifteenth century.

1. The Views of Historians

Since the beginning of the twentieth century, the progress of this growth has been described over and over again. Emile Mâle, in a masterly work, has made a study of the artistic manifestations of the Christian faith of the Middle Ages. Thanks to a deft choice of some typical scenes from a few chronicles of of the times, J. Huizinga has depicted the social and religious comportment of the people of that time. Interest has also been focused on the evolution of thought, from Thomistic Aristotelianism to the nominalism of Ockham (Etienne Gilson and, more recently, Paul Vignaux and Jacques Chevalier). Lastly, historians of spirituality—such as Joseph Huby, Pierre Rousselot, Félix Vernet, Pierre Pourrat, François Vandenbroucke— have inventoried the growth of devotions, extolled the writings on mysticism, or striven to discern the tendencies of a spiritual orientation that was considered to be innovative, and even dangerous: did not the devotio moderna lead to free inquiry, in any case to pietism?

But a description is not an explanation. The attempts to explain the religious phenomenon at the end of the Middle Ages have been varied, partial, and somewhat brief. The Hundred Years War (which extended officially from 1337 to 1453) with its many episodes, the Black Plague of 1348-49 and its numerous aftereffects, brought about unprecedented social upheavals, such as a catastrophic depopulation and premature social progress. The great Western Schism (1378-1429) divided the ecclesiastical hierarchy, the heads of governments, and the faithful. And lastly, there was a breach or intellectual dissociation between theology, faith, and mystical experience. All these factors made a considerable impression and retained the attention of the medieval chroniclers and the historians of our time.[2]

Certainly the psychological and perhaps the religious effect of cataclysms is a turning in upon oneself which leads to pessimism. Is this an explanation that accounts for the apparently disparate flowering of the religious manifestations of this period, such as more and more realistic *Crucifixions* and the sometimes shocking vagrant preaching, the *Danses Macabres* or the *Mystical Lamb* of John Van Eyck, the *Riches Heures* of the Duke de Berry and the *Mysteries of the Passion,* the contemplative sorrow of the *Pietas* and the *Burials,* the naïveté or affected winsomeness of *Virgins with Child,* or the return of the Italian artists to antiquity, the religious or rustic illumination of the *Books of Hours,* the multiplicity of guilds and the success of the Third Orders, the various kinds of *Meditations on the Life of Christ* that extend from the end of the thirteenth century up to the appearance of the *Imitation of Christ* in the first quarter of the fifteenth, and, lastly, the mystical writings: those of the Rhineland, of a Catherine of Siena in Italy, of John Ruysbroeck and of the "good cook," John of Leeuwen in the Low Countries, or of Julian of Norwich in England, and of Gerson in France?

To understand "the tenderness of the new times"[3] or their violence, their riches, and their dynamism, we must relate them to the tradition that gave rise to them and examine the vital surge that sustained them.

The "mental attitudes" of medieval Christianity, which Georges Duby studied recently, shed new light on the arts, the movement of ideas, the history of society, and the manifestations of religious life. Though in continuity with the past, they show such innovative tendencies that the author sees in the century and a half extending from 1280 to 1440, the "foundations of a new humanism," at once lay and Christian.

The monastic world shaped the Christian life of the mass of the faithful as well as artistic creation for a long time. Next, the intellectual influence of the universities gradually asserted itself. In the fourteenth and fifteenth centuries, the heads of government, the lords, the bourgeois, the members of the urban communities, corporations, and guilds, and lastly the people themselves seem to have become more and more conscious of their personality. Christian life also became conscious of itself.

Confronted with the dark forces of nature or of "supernature," man floundered. His bonds with God had in the past been more communitarian, but the community was often gregarious; now it was becoming personalized. The Christian contemplated Christ living and acting, as the "Meditations" and the statuary of his church represented Him. He wanted "to see" his God, a God close to him, a God who had lived and suffered like him, and through whom he hoped to conquer death, that hideous death that constantly flouted him. Man at the end of the Middle Ages turned from Christ in glory, from Christ the Teacher, to the Infant Christ, Christ working, healing, suffering, dying, and conquering death.

Lastly, and this is an important consideration, the religious Middle Ages witnessed a positive forward thrust of woman. The male religious Orders had their feminine homologues— Poor Clares, Dominicans, Augustinians, hospital Sisters of all kinds, and Carmelites in the fifteenth century—but also their male and female Third Orders. This forward thrust was to end in giving the faith more human and more familiar accents in seeing the person of Christ, His life and His Passion with the eyes of the heart, and at the same time in fostering what Hilda Graef calls "the feminine mystique." The medieval "intimate friendship" *(familiaritas)* was necessarily tinged with a certain femininity.

2. Sources and Initiators

Every study of medieval Christian life and spirituality, and more particularly of the devotion and contemplation of Christ's humanity, would be cut off from its essential basis were it not preceded by the presentation of the spiritual doctrine of St. Anselm of Canterbury (†1109), of St. Bernard (†1153), and of St. Bonaventure (†1274). Medieval Christology is theirs; the devotional themes and emphases from the thirteenth to the fifteenth centuries take up and develop their teaching; the road that leads to mystical union is the one they outlined and experienced. Before these great teachers figure the personalities of St. Augustine and St. Gregory the Great.

These sources are discerned either implicitly or clearly through the devotional and mystical medieval texts, but perhaps with less clarity and intensity in the speculative Rhineland-

Flemish tradition. The doctrinal and spiritual continuity is there, straightforward, clear, and evident, despite the blurs that the brutal or sentimental exuberance of the Middle Ages creates. The reader may wish to consult the DS for the doctrine of these masters under their respective names. Reinstated in this doctrinal soil, the resultant developments will seem neither mediocre nor aberrant; they will give rise to the various forms of full blooming of the teaching and example of these initiators.

"The inspired initiator of the Middle Ages is St. Bernard," says F. Vernet, and he adds that with John of Fécamp (eleventh century) there is "the whole cult of Christ's humanity in its embryonic stage."[4] The same can also be said of Aelred of Rievaulx (†1166).[5] A. Wilmart, for his part, has shown what medieval piety owed to St. Anselm.

St. Francis of Assisi (†1226) was also the initiator of a new way of living the Christian life: both more "literal" ("the gospel of the letter") and more "free," with the freedom of the children of God, more in contact with creation ("Brother Sun," "Sister Moon," "Sister Water," "Brother Fire"), and closer to those who were in pain and suffering (kissing the leper). To reveal a Christ who understands the life of men, helps them and brings them the perfect joy of childhood and of the cross: such was Francis' message. He made man "see" creation and he made man "see" the Lord (the crib of Greccio in 1223 and the stigmata of 1226). Certainly, a considerable number of his admirers went no further than the "fioretti" (the work dates from 1330-1340; there are still more than eighty mss. extant and sixteen incunabular editions). These same admirers hardly surmised the exigencies of Franciscan asceticism or Francis' mystical experience. The saint had opened a way that was both more human and more Christian by which all could follow Christ. And many wanted to commit themselves to it. It was the golden age of Third Orders, religious Orders rivaling in another to set up fervent associations which in addition would assure them recruits.

The posthumous glory of Francis, his *fioretti* and his spirit, the ardor and zeal of his sons and daughters—the Friars Minor, the Poor Clares, and the tertiaries—drew Christians toward a naïve and profound familiarity with the supernatural world:

Christ, His mother, and the saint, a familiarity which expressed
itself in the candor and realism of simple souls.

St. Bonaventure was a theologian and a mystic. Medieval
writers refer to his writings as much as they do to those of St.
Bernard. They also attribute a number of treatises to him that
could claim kinship with his spirit, his teaching on meditation
and contemplation, or devotion to Christ, as well as on the
ways of divine vision and ecstasy, just as they did to the
master of Clairvaux. This accounts for the importance and dif-
fusion of his sermons and treatises, of his divine Offices and
prayers, whether it be the sermon-like treatise on the "five
feasts of the Infant Jesus," the Office of the Passion, or the
Praise of the Holy Cross, the Word of Life, or the *Mystical
Vine,* or the outstanding and official biography of his master, St. Francis. Bonaventure's influence was preponderant up
to the best representations of the *Devotio Moderna* at the end
of the Middle Ages.

3. Language and Morals

Very erudite linguistic studies with good glossaries have been
made on medieval poetry. But we have not even crossed the
threshold of such scholarship regarding the popular, literary, or
scholarly language used in every day life in the secular or religious theater, in sermons, in literature, or in the schools. In-
dependently of the devotional or mystical vocabulary of the
spiritual authors, of which the DS gives samples, we find in
the texts that we are studying in this chapter courtly language,
allegorical language, and the language of the street.

The simplicity of the common language moved hearts, and
so it is the one used in the Mysteries and the Plays, and sometimes even in the paraliturgies. The Virgin was supposed to
please and move the spectators of the mystery of the Nativity
(fifteenth century) when she presented the Infant to the Magi.
"My lords, see, I hold the Son of God and my child in my lap;/
He is the One who upholds the whole world." To which Gaspar
answered: "Lady, our very great thanks./ Has anyone ever
seen a more beautiful son?"

Whether these allegories rocked the people in their dreams
or severely criticized their entourage, they liked them. If it is
true, for example, that "the conflict between Justice and Mercy

dominates the cyclic dramas of the Passion in the fifteenth century,"[6] this debate had been popularized by the *Meditations on the Life of Christ*,[7] which re-echoed and amplified St. Bernard's first sermon on the Annunciation so well that the debate is met throughout the Middle Ages in didactic poetry, scholastic treatises, meditations and collections of sermons and even in the *Spiritual Exercises* of St. Ignatius of Loyola (1548).[8] This allegorical language no doubt made it easier to transform the Mysteries into satires. The popular preachers, with their moralist bent, thoroughly enjoyed themselves at the expense of their listeners, of "the establishment," and of all society.

To the "imaginary in (popular) devotion," G. Duby explains, there corresponded "the imaginary in courtliness" and chivalry; to the representation of the saints, "the cortege of nine brave Knights";[9] to the sacred aesthetic, a "secular aesthetic"; to the sepulchers which were "an act of edification and of humility," other tombs that ostentatiously manifested "a social success, the victory of man and his glory";[10] to the call for a "Christian survival" there was joined the call to a "secular survival." "The refinements of courtly pleasure were introduced in the image of piety,"[11] just as the worst excesses follow the most refined actions. The two trends, the two yearnings, meet each other, penetrate each other, and contradict each other in the crudeness of manorial or popular mores, and cause "Christianity" to lose its cohesion and sense. If man became more conscious of himself at the end of the Middle Ages, he was torn "between the imitation of Christ and possessing the world."[12]

These tendencies and yearnings undoubtedly help us to get a better grasp of the pathetic art of the man of this period, his tormented life, his unpolished and passionate devotions. They make Christianity loom as a religion of the people which "urged the laity to pray themselves, to pronounce the words of the sacred texts themselves and, if they were capable, to read them alone and to understand them." Their Christian life passed into their everyday life.[13]

B. Devotions to the Humanity of Christ

1. General Remarks

Medieval devotions were collective or private. The guilds

had their own, as did the parishes and the monasteries. The
............................eir own.

Maintain a clear conscience before God and man
Acts 24:16

essed in very different ways: the
s and pilgrimages, liturgical or
rticular acts of piety, or art in
e of the cathedrals and chapels,
vs, tombs, sculpture and painting,
eater and literature.

d to another, from one region to
asp; to generalize their character-
ometimes it is the crudeness, the
that strike or perhaps shock us.
t Assisi at the end of the thirteenth
ts-at-the-Pillar or the *Crucifixions*
of Issenheim, etc.) at the begin-
manifest it. The brutal macera-
terary or vivid descriptions of the
e cross, the detailed account of the
flagellation, which the mystics re-
trations of the preachers: all echo
grace and the gentleness of the
Jesus, the ecstatic recollection of
erds and the Magi, the appeased
beauty, interior silence or violence,
culture, all this we find in the ex-
ns.

it "many works of art of the four-
tely conceived as visual and read-
ody of doctrine."[14] The *Mystery*
o prolong on the stage the teach-
eight of the pulpit by having the
them be mimed. As E. Delaruelle
instruct asserts itself at every mo-
y at the end of the Middle Ages.
on forms that lent themselves to
ast they ran the risk of diverting
o the accidental. In any case, such
image, the ever ambiguous yet
oday we are ill at ease with the
terminology of devotions,' and we hold responsible those

who use it and those who practice devotions. It is important
to remind ourselves of the multiple meanings of this terminology. The reader may be wise to refer to the articles in the DS
entitled *Devotio* and *Dévotions*. The increased number of devotions at the end of the Middle Ages were for that period what
audio-visual means are for us today: "close-ups" of favorite
scenes from the life and especially the Passion of Christ, of
His person, His behavior, His actions, and His body; "film-
strips," to which the actors of the liturgical plays and the
Mysteries, or the preachers, added the sound effects. In this
context, the naïve and in some way the primitive piety of the
faithful, often helpless before the events, is far from always
deserving the banderillas of an Erasmus,[16] the mockeries of a
Rabelais, or the disgusted airs of more "enlightened" generations. In its own way, this piety recognized in Christ, whether
child or suffering, the God-Man who was born and suffered for
the salvation of the world.

Medieval devotions to Christ's humanity have three centers
of interest: the childhood, the Passion, and the Eucharist.

2. Devotions to the Childhood and to the Public Life

Devotion to the crib was a manifestation of the faith of
Francis of Assisi in the Incarnation of the Word. We have already spoken of its success. The same must be said of the
devotion to the Childhood.

Devotion to the Name of Jesus is somewhat the contribution
of St. Bernardine of Siena (†1444); so much did he preach
it that it was inscribed in hearts and engraved on monuments,
thus popularizing the acronym IHS.[17] To repeat and venerate
this name was to recall to mind and venerate the name par excellence, the name of our Saviour, as a child calls his mother,
or a wife her husband. The devotion was approved by Gregory
X at the ecumenical Council of Lyon in 1274. The papal
decretal was nothing more than the consecration of a devotion
that St. Anselm already knew, which "welled up from the mysticism of St. Bernard and of St. Francis,"[18] and continued to
spread. Friar Guibert of Tournai (†1284), who attended the
Council of Lyon in the company of St. Bonaventure, wrote a
treatise on the Holy Name which is a series of sermons addressed to the Friars Minor on this theme.[19]

had their own, as did the parishes and the monasteries. The individual faithful also had their own.

These devotions were expressed in very different ways: the popular piety of processions and pilgrimages, liturgical or para-liturgical ceremonies, particular acts of piety, or art in all its forms: the architecture of the cathedrals and chapels, statuary, stained glass windows, tombs, sculpture and painting, miniatures and xylography, theater and literature.

The trends from one period to another, from one region to another, remain difficult to grasp; to generalize their characteristics would be dangerous. Sometimes it is the crudeness, the violence, and a coarse realism that strike or perhaps shock us. The *Crucifixion* of Cimabue at Assisi at the end of the thirteenth century portends it: the *Christs-at-the-Pillar* or the *Crucifixions* of Grünewald (the reredos of Issenheim, etc.) at the beginning of the sixteenth century manifest it. The brutal macerations by the flagellants, the literary or vivid descriptions of the tragic scenes of the way of the cross, the detailed account of the blows of the scourge at the flagellation, which the mystics reveal, and the pathetic demonstrations of the preachers: all echo it. At other times it is the grace and the gentleness of the *Madonnas* and of the *Infant Jesus,* the ecstatic recollection of the *Adorations* of the shepherds and the Magi, the appeased sorrow of the *Pietás.* Grace, beauty, interior silence or violence, earthly realism and lack of culture, all this we find in the expression of medieval devotions.

Yet, it can be affirmed that "many works of art of the fourteenth century were deliberately conceived as visual and readable representations of a body of doctrine."[14] The *Mystery Plays,* in turn, sought only to prolong on the stage the teachings proclaimed from the height of the pulpit by having the faithful mime them or watch them be mimed. As E. Delaruelle has shown, "the concern to instruct asserts itself at every moment"[15] in the theatrical play at the end of the Middle Ages.

Sometimes devotions took on forms that lent themselves to magic or superstition; at least they ran the risk of diverting attention from the essential to the accidental. In any case, such was the problem with the image, the ever ambiguous yet indispensable mediation. Today we are ill at ease with the terminology of "devotions," and we hold responsible those

who use it and those who practice devotions. It is important
to remind ourselves of the multiple meanings of this terminology. The reader may be wise to refer to the articles in the DS
entitled *Devotio* and *Dévotions.* The increased number of devotions at the end of the Middle Ages were for that period what
audio-visual means are for us today: "close-ups" of favorite
scenes from the life and especially the Passion of Christ, of
His person, His behavior, His actions, and His body; "film-
strips," to which the actors of the liturgical plays and the
Mysteries, or the preachers, added the sound effects. In this
context, the naïve and in some way the primitive piety of the
faithful, often helpless before the events, is far from always
deserving the banderillas of an Erasmus,[16] the mockeries of a
Rabelais, or the disgusted airs of more "enlightened" generations. In its own way, this piety recognized in Christ, whether
child or suffering, the God-Man who was born and suffered for
the salvation of the world.

Medieval devotions to Christ's humanity have three centers
of interest: the childhood, the Passion, and the Eucharist.

2. Devotions to the Childhood and to the Public Life

Devotion to the crib was a manifestation of the faith of
Francis of Assisi in the Incarnation of the Word. We have already spoken of its success. The same must be said of the
devotion to the Childhood.

Devotion to the Name of Jesus is somewhat the contribution
of St. Bernardine of Siena (†1444); so much did he preach
it that it was inscribed in hearts and engraved on monuments,
thus popularizing the acronym IHS.[17] To repeat and venerate
this name was to recall to mind and venerate the name par excellence, the name of our Saviour, as a child calls his mother,
or a wife her husband. The devotion was approved by Gregory
X at the ecumenical Council of Lyon in 1274. The papal
decretal was nothing more than the consecration of a devotion
that St. Anselm already knew, which "welled up from the mysticism of St. Bernard and of St. Francis,"[18] and continued to
spread. Friar Guibert of Tournai (†1284), who attended the
Council of Lyon in the company of St. Bonaventure, wrote a
treatise on the Holy Name which is a series of sermons addressed to the Friars Minor on this theme.[19]

The *Jubilus,* said to be of St. Bernard, or the *Jesu dulcis memoria,* of which successive compositions were to have from forty-two to seventy-nine strophes, was composed at the beginning of the thirteenth century. This poem, very likely the work of an English Cistercian, knew an extraordinary vogue. A. Wilmart noted eighty-eight manuscripts of it from the thirteenth to the fifteenth centuries. It quickly entered into the tradition of the popular piety with which it harmonized. It was rather naturally connected with sacramental Communion; it was also adapted to the recitation of a kind of liturgical Office according to the hours of the night and day. At the same time it served in a general way to spread devotion to the "most sweet" name of the Saviour of men and became an integral part of a regular and approved Office when the feast of the Most Holy Name was established (fifteenth century) under the influence of the Friars Minor.[20]

This devotion was popular in England. Richard Rolle (†1349), for example, praised the name of Jesus in his *Commentary on the Canticle.* The name, Richard said, "purifies, wounds with love and makes one contemplative." He himself invoked it frequently.[21] In Italy, at the same period, John Colombini allowed his companions to be called Jesuati in honor of the name of Jesus.

It would be fitting at this juncture to mention "the prayer to Jesus," which is closely connected with devotion to the name of Jesus. Familiar and very dear to Oriental Christians, it will be given special treatment in the article *Prière à Jésus* in the DS.

Let us note that among all the names given Christ by the piety of the Middle Ages, this or that appellation made theologians knit their eyebrows. To designate Christ who begets men unto divine life by such names as "Father," or "Mother," did not in the least shock the Christians of those times. The spiritual maternity of Christ, considered in a kind of "affectionate speculation or speculative affection," according to the expression of J. de Ghellinck, was already attested to by St. Anselm (†1109), and we see it again in the fifteenth century in the Carthusian Dominic of Prussia (†1460). However, it seems that Julian of Norwich (†1342)[22] explained it at much greater length and with the greatest simplicity.[23]

3. Devotions to the Passion

a) A few characteristics

The piety of the faithful at the end of the Middle Ages was particularly attracted by the Passion, Christ's sufferings and death, by the instruments of the Passion and the cross. The arts, the plays, the *Mysteries,* the preaching, spiritual treatises, and the *Books of Hours,* all testify to this. Whereas the spirituality of the Crosier Order, which was founded in the thirteenth century, manifests "signs of a special devotion to the holy cross and to the Passion of the Saviour,"[24] the people themselves were looking for an explanation of their suffering and help to live it. They found them in the example of Christ who bore the suffering and agony of the world and of everyone, and who gave, as He left the tomb victorious, the assurance of having conquered death (see Lk 24:26). The many-sided devotion to the Passion shows how man is moved in the depths of his sorrowful and innermost being. That this devotion was here and there attended by morbid elements and an exaggerated sorrow is obvious. It is also obvious that it was directed to Christ, God and man, who redeemed the world by His suffering and cross and who rose from the tomb.

Two remarks of an exegetical and psychological order may throw light on the nature of these devotions. In the Middle Ages the texts traditionally applied to Christ were understood in their most physical sense. Without insisting on the figures of the ox and the donkey, of which Isaiah speaks (Is 1:3), that henceforth form part of the crib, the same physical sense applies to the narratives of the Passion. The Psalms, the Lamentations of Jeremiah, Isaiah, and the Evangelists are taken literally .

In view of this exegesis, we find recurring characteristics during the entire Middle Ages and even beyond; the Passion of Christ is *necessarily* "the most ignominious, the most cruel, the most general and the longest." This is what, for example, St. Bonaventure develops as a traditional datum.[25] There is no greater ignominy than the Passion and death in the circumstances that accompany it, "among the wicked" (Is 53:9). The most sensitive and most perfect constitution, as was that of Christ's in virtue of the axiom "the nobility of one's constitution corresponds to the nobility of one's soul," entails the keenest and most general suffering, "from the sole of his foot . . ." (Is 1:6); the Passion began with birth. No passion or suffering equals that of our Lord: "Look and see if there is any sorrow like my sorrow" (Lam 1:12).[26]

In this setting, the authors of meditations, preachers, and artists were able to embellish according to their imagination or devotion. But, at the same time, from these Scripture texts and from the unfathomable example of the Passion of Christ and from the compassion of His mother, there arose an extraordinary respect and insatiable desire of imitation by conformity, which the title of chapter thirteen of the *Little Book of Eternal Wisdom* of Henry Suso correctly describes: "Of the infinite nobility of temporal suffering." Many texts of medieval authors, of Suso, Tauler, Thomas à Kempis, and of many others corroborate this. The crucified life of St. Lydwina of Schiedam (†1433) was an instance of this kind of pity.

b) Principal devotions

The *Way of the Cross* takes up the narrative of the Passion and enables one to contemplate its principal scenes by advancing or stopping with Christ (steps and stations), and by suffering with Him (agony, blows, falls, crucifixion). This ascent to Calvary is a spiritual pilgrimage that moved hearts and sustained faith: "He entered once for all into the Holy Place, taking not the blood of goats and calves but His own blood, thus securing an eternal redemption" (Heb 9:12).

This walk with Christ gives us a better understanding of how the Christian could become spiritually inclined toward and attached to a particular event, a particular attitude, a particular word of Christ, and how new devotional aspects, whether individual or collective, could come into being. And so devotion to Christ tied to the pillar ("the Christ of pity"), to the Holy Face, to the wounds, and to Christ's side appear. If there is not, properly speaking, veneration paid to Christ's words on the cross, we know with what veneration people meditated upon them.

All the enthusiasm of the devotion of the faithful was directed to *Christ on the cross*: contemplation of Christ dying, fervent attention to His words and to His being taken down from the cross, contemplation of the cross and of the crucifix, and lastly compassion because this is inseparable from the crucifixion. The cross, the sacred emblem par excellence of the redemption, was reproduced everywhere, on and in sacred and public buildings; it was honored in private homes and carried on one's person. This completely spontaneous devotion was the outcome of the liturgical adoration of the cross and of its constant liturgical use. It had proliferated in countless *Offices of the Passion* and *of the Compassion,* which the faithful liked to recite or to psalmodize from memory. The "passion clocks" were another form that was popular at the end of the Middle Ages: meditation of the Passion was distributed according to the hours of the Office and the hours of the day by means of a clock. In this way the mystery of the redemption was ever present to the heart of the Christian.

The devotion to the *wounds* of Christ was undoubtedly one of the most characteristic of the period we are concerned with; "fully developed at the height of the thirteenth century,"[27] it was common to many of the faithful and at the same time put them on the path of the mystical life. According to the accounts of visions from which the influence of the mysticism of numbers is not absent, the number of blows Christ received in the course of the Passion is impressive and provoked countless prayers. The devotional movement, however, only retained the wound in the feet and in the hands, that of the side and often that of the head crowned with thorns. Those who put this devotion into practice earnestly recommended it. Among these were St. Bernard,[28] William of Saint-Thierry,[29] the German mystics of the fourteenth century, for example, Henry Suso and John Tauler, and anonymous writers of the same school. "One transport of love toward the holy wounds of our Lord," John Tauler declared with some humor to the Dominican nuns, "is more precious before God than all the stops of an organ, all the chiming of clocks, all the beautiful chants, and all the chasubles with embroidered coats-of-arms."[30] Let us add that the apocryphal letters of Tauler repeatedly offer exercises of devotion to the wounds. The *Institutions* of pseudo-Tauler also speak of them.

Devotion to the *blood* of Christ is bound up with that of His wounds. Relics—of questionable authenticity—of the Precious

Blood brought back by the Crusaders, gave new life to the devotion. The "procession of the Precious Blood" at Bruges was solemnized from the beginning of the fourteenth century with exceptional popular success: its folkloric aspects do not conceal the piety that animates it, and it is certainly much more than an "interesting spectacle that religiously embellished medieval life," as J. Toussaert would have it.[31] On this point, he seems to forget the exigencies of being an historian. More will be said later about the importance and the place of devotion to the blood of Christ when we treat of the mysticism of Catherine of Siena.

The devotion of the faithful seems to have been hardly affected by the somewhat useless quarrels that arose in the fifteenth century between the Dominican and Franciscan scholastic theologians regarding the lawfulness of adoration of Christ's outpoured blood. Their differing views were defended before Roman congregations and Popes.

4. Devotions to the Eucharist and to the Heart of Christ

These devotions are directly related to the devotions to the Passion. Devotion to the Eucharistic Christ, whom the faithful wanted "to see," to sing, contemplate, and adore, underwent considerable development in the Middle Ages. Devotion to the Heart of Christ seems, nevertheless, to have been stronger among mystics and in the religious Orders than with the Christian people.[32]

5. Evolution of Devotions

Art, like liturgical texts and ceremonies, and books of private prayer, is a good test of the evolution of the characteristics of devotion to Christ at the end of the Middle Ages. By way of example, we might recall the representations of the crucifixion, as explained in the remarkable book of Paul Thoby.[33]

To go from the glorious Christ of the High Middle Ages in its Byzantine stylization, "crystallized into an eternal type,"[34] to the sorrowful Christ of the mystics of the thirteenth and fourteenth centuries, then to the bloodstained Christ of the fifteenth, gives rise to astonishment, and even lack of understanding or rejection. The "tendency to pathos" became more marked very quickly: the body of the Crucified One sagged, became longer, hung lopsidedly, and even became transformed into an anatomical study. The crown of thorns appeared on the head of the Crucified when St. Louis the King received the "holy crown" (1239); it made the head of Christ bleed. From then on, the manner of depicting blood on the body of Christ became ever more moving, but was not always appropriate. The crucifixion tended actually to represent "the image of pain and death," that pain and death which are the common lot of all men who are haunted by every peril, and who, feeling the need to bring their God closer to their miserable state, sometimes do so in an excessive manner.

It would indeed be of no avail to attempt to present the evolution of the *Crucifixions* during the two centuries that now engage our attention; its wide diversity would call for necessary explanations. Fra Angelico (†1455) perpetuated at St. Mark's in Florence "the unchanging image of Christ as the divine beauty."[35] Yet, before him, around 1390, an anonymous master painted a *Crucifixion* in which the blood trickles (the Museum of Florence), whereas at the height of the fourteenth century one of the most tragic of Christs, called the Christ of Bajasse (hospice of Brioude, Haute-Loire), was carved in wood for lepers. This carving bore "not only the stamp of the sufferings of the Passion but of a long misery, like that of a leper."[36] It was at this same time that the German school with its wooden Christ of St. Maria im Kapitol at Cologne or the "Devout Christ" of the cathedral of Perpignan (1307) drew its inspiration from "the boldest excesses" and from an "unbridled realism."[37]

If this realism was always spectacular throughout the fifteenth century, new elements attenuated it. The miniatures, those of the *Rohan Hours,* for example, at the beginning of the century adhered to a healthy realism, as did the *Crucifixion* of Perugino at Perugia in the second half of the century. Emotion, however, tended to subside, and theological and mystical influence began to appear. Already in the fourteenth century, but especially in the fifteenth, the sign of the redemption in the form of large wooden Christs surrounded by various gospel personages was erected on a triumphal beam in the center of the church choirs. The Christs of pity were often accompanied by profoundly sorrowful, but circumspect and contemplative *Pietàs*, or by Christs at the winepress of sorrow. The "fountain of life" or of pity collected the precious blood that flows from the Saviour's wounds to wash and take away sin. The God-Man and man the sinner met each other.

This evolution of the fourteenth and fifteenth centuries, which art forces us to note, had its beginnings even before St. Bernard. It nevertheless seems that the orientation toward this impressive realism was due especially to the influence of St. Francis of Assisi. The chroniclers took pleasure in describing as many as seven manifestations of Jesus crucified to Francis; this made him "the incomparable mystic of Calvary," "the knight of the Crucified One," according to the expression of Thomas of Celano, which the *Fioretti* popularized. Francis wanted to be conformed to the crucified Christ "because Christ hung naked on the cross, in poverty and pain."[38] Lastly, the privilege of the stigmata made the Poverello the herald of Christ Crucified. To Francis' example let us add the teaching of Bonaventure. Etienne Gilson remarks: "St. Bonaventure's Virgin at Calvary is already the Virgin of the following centuries."[39]

The accounts of the visions of the mystics, especially of Saints Angela of Foligno (†1309) and Bridget of Sweden (†1373), give and sanction the realistic descriptions from which the artists draw their inspiration, which the theatrical plays and preachers expand upon; but the "Meditations" and the "Lives of Christ" comment freely on Isaiah's texts and the Passions of the Evangelists. And lastly we can say that "the history of the crucifix ... is the unfolding of all the creations dedicated to the drama of Calvary ... with the theological doctrines that inspired them, the historical events that influenced them, the geographical and ethnic elements that modified them, and the religious and secular literature that propagated them." Whatever may be said of their sources, "all these *Crucifixions* retell ... the deep faith and the immense love that inspired them."[40]

6. Devotions and the Daily Life of the Christian

It would not be out of place to present these different devotions in the daily reality of the Christian's life. The chronicles and the memoirs of individuals are reticent on this point. The only useful information we might find would be in the inventories of libraries—Books of Hours or miniatures, for example —and objects of piety or of ornamentation such as tableaux, statuettes, crosses, and pendants. These are clues whose importance we must beware of over-evaluating. Were they the sign of devotion or of a level of economic and social life?

The German mystic Henry Suso (†1366) describes his devotions. The case of this Dominican is instructive because he had disciples to whom he recommended his own practices of piety and because he represented a fervent milieu of male and female religious faithful.

Suso multiplied devotions to Christ's humanity. We know, for example, that he cut the monogram IHS on his chest; material that he had touched was even distributed imprudently. One could see in his chapel "the loveable name of Jesus well illuminated and adorned with maxims to stimulate hearts." A small group was formed that honored the name of Jesus every day by appropriate prayers. "I beg you, Lord," Suso prayed "to stamp yourself deeper in the depths of my heart... in such a way that you will never again separate yourself from it."[41]

In the chapter room and in the monastery church, Henry Suso followed the itinerary of the *Way of the Cross;* he accompanied Christ, genuflected and kissed His footprints; he prayed and stood aside, "picturing to himself mentally the different scenes with as much precision as he could"; or if he were in choir with the community, he made "the Way of the Cross interiorly."[42]

He had a special devotion to the *cross.* "On the outskirts of a small town he venerated a wooden crucifix housed in a small chapel, as is customary in certain countries."[43]

He honored the entire *Passion* by the practice of a hundred prostrations *(venia),* accompanied by appropriate meditations and prayers; the practice became known and spread.[44] As B. Lavaud explains in his Introduction, "a prostration to honor an aspect of the Passion, a sorrow, a word or a sentiment of the heart of Christ crucified or of His Mother, and the formulation of a desire suggested by the event that is being contemplated is an act of complete prayer in which the body and the higher faculties of the soul harmoniously concur."[45]

Suso's devotion to Christ's *wounds* was sincere and profound. He gave himself the discipline to the point that "he looked like Christ when he was cruelly scourged." Furthermore, he wore a cross with iron nails on his back, day and night for eight years "in special memory of all Christ's wounds and of His five signs of love."[46]

If it were necessary to conclude this chapter with a remark on the "new outpouring of Christian piety" in the Middle Ages, it would suffice to recall to mind with André Wilmart "the first principle of every sudden and yet natural blooming, the one thanks to which medieval religion remained closely linked with the preceding ages, namely, the cult of the cross. The most complete manifestation of the cult of the cross, if I am not mistaken, appears in the eleventh century, its foundations having undoubtedly been laid down for quite some time. Rather numerous prayers since the ninth century show how, apart from the liturgy, there began to be meditations on the sufferings of the Savior. The liturgy had even answered this need much earlier by the solemn ceremony of the adoration of the Cross on Good Friday. But it was also around the eleventh century that it became enriched, at least in certain countries, with even more dramatic manifestations of the divestiture of the cross and of the Host, destined to further accentuate the triumph of Easter."[47]

C. Devotions, Mystery Plays, and Preaching

The aim of the devotions we have just set forth was a more authentic knowledge of Christ, a greater attachment to His service and person, and a deeper love. Surely, the devout person runs the risk of not going beyond, or of imperfectly going beyond, the vivid representation of his devotion and of performing more or less magical and superstitious actions. God alone knows the number of devout persons who fail to avoid this excess. Did the Middle Ages succeed better than the twentieth century?

To answer this question, one ought to know what instruction the faithful received. Now it is clear that in using these very concrete devotions, the Church through the liturgy and the religious literature of the fourteenth and fifteenth centuries was trying to lead the faithful to God through meditation on and contemplation of Christ. But there were various paths leading to this: plays and Passions, the writings of mystics or simply devotional treatises, and preaching. From the diversity of these forms of teaching, we would like to retain what has bearing on the Mystery Plays and the collections of sermons, for both were accessible to the greater number of people. Let us first draw the reader's attention to the prayers of devotion.

1. Prayers of Devotion, Liturgy, and Common Language

The bonds between liturgy and private prayer are dealt with in a very clear way in the article *Dévotions* in the DS.[48] We shall, therefore, limit ourselves to one or two questions. If the organization of the liturgy, which with the reform of Pius V became inflexible, paradoxically contributed to the multiplicity of devotions, another reason furthered their growth in the Middle Ages: the use of liturgical Latin, at least in the West. Few of the faithful, with the exception of the learned scholars, knew Latin; they preferred to understand their prayers and express them in their mother tongue, without for all of that being looked upon as Waldensians or Lollards. "In the fourteenth century," J. Bazire states, "in England gentlemen and ladies prayed their devotions in English or in French, whereas the female religious who knew how to read recited their Office in Latin, which they did not ordinarily understand."[49] There were, however, convents where religious recited their Office in their mother tongue. In the fifteenth century, John Busch censured the convents of Augustinian Sisters who did this.[50]

2. Liturgical Plays, Mystery Plays, and Laudi

The end of the Middle Ages was a period of truly rich popular religious teaching. This teaching was effected by plentiful and ordinary audio-visual means, which printing partially supplanted in the fifteenth century. It was, in fact, by pictures, plays, mimes, theatrical representations, liturgical chant, and songs based on contemporary melodies, and even choreography, that the teaching of the preachers, and of the clerical scenario writers, was retransmitted and amplified. In this way they directly reached the actor, the spectator, and the audience.

As É. Delaruelle, following K. Young and G. Cohen, has

shown, the liturgy from the tenth to the thirteenth century stressed its dramatic aspect and incorporated para-liturgies, especially into the liturgies of Christmas and of the Resurrection. The liturgical dramas, then the semi-liturgical ones, formed "a transition toward the *play* or the *miracle* somewhat later," and then the *mystery*.[51]

Across Europe—in Germany, England, Spain, Italy, the Low Countries, and in France—the "mysteries," adapted to the people and written in their language, assumed an even greater importance from the fourteenth century on. The mystery (*ministerium,* or function, at the beginning of the fifteenth century has itself the meaning of representation) in the beginning restricted itself to dramatizing in "live, animated tableaus" a biblical narrative. It was gradually transformed into a theatrical play with abundant and modern accessories. It readily took in the entire plan of the redemption from the Garden of Eden to the last judgment, as does the oldest mystery that we know of, *The Representation of Adam* (twelfth century), which was presented at Christmas.

Undertaken by confraternities and lay people in great part, the mysteries did not escape the excesses of the genre since their triviality made them first suspect, and finally prohibited. "All creation," L. Petit de Julleville observes, "swarmed at the feet of the Creator: fools, valets, beggars and thieves—a strange retinue, which acted out the Passion of the God-Man."[52]

Be that as it may, beginning with the second half of the fourteenth century, the confraternities (the guilds in England) of the Passion, of the Blessed Sacrament, and others devoted themselves "to the service of instructing the public, and the religious theater changed from Latin to French, English or German."

In truth, "the average person learned the gospel once again" in the great Passion—as someone has said, "the Passions of theologians," for example, the *Passion of Palatinus* of the fourteenth century, the *Passion of Semur,* famous for its modern staging, but also for its violence, its buffoonery, and also for its tenderness; the *Passion of Arras* by Eustache Mercadé (around 1430); the *Passion* of Arnoul Gréban (1449) which was "imitated indefinitely," and whose focus of interest was more the resurrection than the Passion. In addition to these

Passions, we should also recall the *Mysteries of the Resurrection* of the second half of the fourteenth century, the "Nativities," the *Miracles of Notre Dame,* which are inseparable from them, such as the *Advocacie Notre Dame* (1406) or the *Mystery of the Assumption,* as well as the Provençal *Mysteries of the Passion, of the Ascension,* the *Plays of Corpus Christi, of the Sacred Host,* and so forth.

The *Christmas Plays,* the *Passion Plays,* or the *Plays of the Resurrection* enjoyed an astonishing success in Germany in the fifteenth century. At that same time there were also the plays of the *Childhood of Christ,* of the *Ascension,* etc. The most peculiar one is certainly the *Ludus utilis ad devotionem simplicium peragendus die Corporis Christi* (1391). In England at this same time, the *Mysteries on the Day of Corpus Christi* were important and popular; at least sixty of them are known of today.

The popular religious theater traces its origin to the vogue of the *laudi* that flourished in Italy from the thirteenth century. Here again, Francis of Assisi was an initiator. The confraternities gathered together to sing them and make them better known. Profoundly evangelical, the *laudi* extol Christ the Son of man, Mary, his mother, a woman of the people, and also the Eucharistic Christ and the cross. The literary genre was transposed to the stage and transformed into *sacra rappresentazione* (sacred portrayal), which reached its apogee in the fifteenth century.

In its different forms this theater had, as a whole, a catechetical, doctrinal, moral, and religious purpose. It expressed the tendencies of popular piety and at the same time strengthened it by setting forth, on the one hand, the bases of its faith and of its devotion to Christ in a concrete way, and, on the other hand, by appealing to the emotions of the people and stirring up their love for this God-Man who thus became their "close friend."[53]

3. Preachers

a) Medieval preaching

It is believed that there were no medieval preachers who did not speak of the mysteries of Christ, and in particular of the cycles of Christmas, of the Passion, and of the Resurrection; likewise, the influence of the preachers on devotions, on their development and their spirit was incalculable. But there is considerable difficulty when it comes to analyzing these sermons. The manuscript texts that have come down to us, like the editions that have been made of them, are mostly adaptations that were composed later, and often in Latin. As a rule these were stenographic reports of sermons that had been improvised or prepared mentally, written by hearers who were sometimes more fervent than competent, whose writings the preacher did not necessarily look over. Because of this important element, it is difficult to recover the inspiration of the thought and form of these sermons, their structure, or the emotional pitch which they reached.

Parish priests had at their disposal "liturgical sermon books" or a "Mirror of Pastors" which, like the "Ami du Clergé" of the twentieth century, gave them sermon models with supplements for the more important cycles. The ms 574 of the Cambrai library (fifteenth century) has, among others, a liturgical sermon book and a *Mirror of Pastors;* it has no less than six sermons for Palm Sunday, an explanation of the "sorrowful week," two sermons for Holy Thursday and Good Friday, five for the Easter feasts, five for Pentecost, and four for the feast of Corpus Christi, and so forth.

We know that there was a reciprocal interplay between the sermons and the mysteries. The latter took up certain parts of the content of the sermons and, with all the means of the stage play, adapted them, magnified them, and at times distorted them. In their turn, the preachers, having become spectators, better realized the tastes of their hearers, the way of speaking to their imagination, to their ears, as well as to their eyes and heart. If their use of artificial divisions—whether Aristotelian or literary—upsets us, their allegorical personifications of the virtues and vices, with their sometimes crude application, must have enormously pleased their congregations; these are as frequent in sermons as they were in the mysteries.

b) A few model preachers of the fifteenth century

We shall limit ourselves here to a few popular preachers (Gerson preached at the university and at the court), and we

shall strive to pinpoint the teaching they gave to the faithful
and their influence on devotional piety. We shall speak of
exhortatory sermons that deal with mystical questions in the
next chapter.

1) The sermons of St. Vincent Ferrer (†1419), a Spanish Dominican, are well known. Those he gave to the Flagellants created a sensation.[54] Of the great number of sermons he
gave before considerable crowds in Spain, France, and elsewhere, all that has been preserved are reports, and to make
matters worse, translated into Latin. Yet the number of editions since 1475 is impressive. It is no less interesting to point
out his devotional themes: the person of Christ, His wounds
and His blood, the crown of thorns, His Eucharistic Body,
prayer and weeping with Christ.

In Sermon 33, St. Vincent says that it is extremely important to "meditate on the works of Christ and to imitate them."
He then presents the thirty principal actions of the life of Christ,
not just the Passion, beginning with the Incarnation up to the
Ascension, that it is fitting to ponder "during the Eucharistic
sacrifice." "Christ's glorified wounds"[55] remain visible in His
glorified body "so that He may carry about with Him the triumph of victory forever." The Lord shows them to the world
as a sign of salvation and to each Christian as a personal call
to conversion. Time and again St. Vincent returns to the
wounds and the crucifixion. In the *Dominicale,* he shows how
the Christian must also "be crucified and receive wounds *ad
instar Christi.*"[56] In his *Festivale,* three sermons are devoted to
the "Holy Cross," Christ's glory, His humility and its degrees,
followed by another sermon that commemorates the feast of
the "crown of Christ," proper to the Dominican Order.[57] The
crown of glory can be obtained only by carrying the crown of
thorns! St. Vincent also preached for the feast of the Exaltation of the Holy Cross.[58] The feast of the Circumcision was
both the feast of Christ's blood and of Christ's name.[59] On the
third Sunday after Easter, the preacher spoke "of the sources
and motives for tears":[60] "When the Christian contemplates
the actions of our Lord's life, for example, the humility of His
Incarnation, the ardor and fervor of devotion *(ardore et fervore
devotionis)* make him forthwith weep." Sermons 111-115 are

devoted to the feast of Corpus Christi, and sermons 5 and 12 of the *Dominicale* to Christ the King.

Vincent Ferrer also held up various titles of Christ to the attention, imitation, and devotion of his audience. Christ is evidently "shepherd."[61] He is also, as St. Augustine had already called Him, "healer."[62] He is likewise a "pilgrim."[63] And lastly, He is "Father." St. Vincent explains it this way: "Christ is the Father of all Christians.... The Church is their mother. He is our Father because He died for us on the cross."[64]

2) A certain number of sermons delivered in French by John Gerson (†1429) have been published recently, and they enable us to become acquainted with his manner of preaching. Gerson did not speak at great length in his sermons about the humanity of Christ and the devotions that honor Him. He was primarily a moral preacher, to the advantage of everyone of his time and of the court of Charles VI. But his sermon on the *Passion of our Lord,* given in 1403, deserves careful study. The simplicity he manifests in it, his sense of human experience, his concern to adapt himself to his audience and to respect them without coercing their feelings, his fidelity in the use of Scripture indeed stand out, in the words of G. Frénaud, "as a synthesis of the most beautiful aspects of medieval piety."[65] Examples abound. Why is he preaching? To put "in the clarity of the true faith the picture and woeful semblance of the good Saviour Jesus who let Himself be so bound for you."[66] He, indeed, utilized his predecessors, Ludolph the Carthusian, Nicolas of Lyra, Saints Bernard and Bonaventure, but above all he employed the literal explanation of Scripture: "When I do not have any unquestionable Scripture text, I use provable conjectures ... without presumptuous assertion, but to arouse to religious devotion."[67] "I will not say such things as are either uncertain or of little profit."[68] It is not that he is against playing on human emotions, but always does so with rare discretion, and the emotion arises precisely from his method. He divided the Passion narrative into twenty-four parts according to the hours of the day in order to teach all men at every moment that to call to the cross of Jesus who died "for all the human family"[69] is their recourse and salva-

tion: "If the world attacks you, if the flesh torments you, if the enemy threatens you, hasten here through true faith, lean on this cross; for by holding it you will not fall, you will not be tormented, you will doubt nothing, you will lose nothing."[70]

In reality, the supreme art of emotion was to describe together from start to finish the Passion of Jesus and that of Mary without distinguishing them. The spiritual tone rose constantly from the call to repentance and conversion before Jesus who "dies shamefully and painfully bound in this way"[71] to the contemplation of the cross: "What will you see there, if not love and absolute charity?"[72] But the Virgin is there at each step, either present or in the background; her attitude commands, so to speak, that of the Saviour's friends, and that of Gerson's audience. See her at the foot of the cross: "Her mother's most piteous and loving heart was wounded and pierced by the sword of the most shameful and sorrowful Passion of her dear Son. Nevertheless, she stood there *(stabat)* straight, so says the gospel; artists who depict her otherwise are not to be believed..."[73] With the same sobriety, the meeting on the morning of the Resurrection is all tenderness and love: "May God save you, Mother."[74]

3) Of St. Bernardine of Siena (†1444) we can retain the sermons on the Last Supper, nos. 54 and 55; on the Passion, no. 56, in which he explains the twenty-eight reasons for the most ignominious *(ignominiosissima)* Passion, the twelve moral and spiritual fruits of the tree of life, and the seven words of Christ on the cross. The *Treatise on the Lord's Passion* had already been given as a sermon. On Easter Tuesday, he delivered a sermon entitled *The Sacred Stigmata of the Glorious Francis.* We might mention two others on the name of Jesus: no. 48, *The Triumphal Title and Exaltation of the Glorious Name of Jesus,* and no. 49, *The Lord's Glorious Name.* Bernardine was not an original thinker. He utilized whole pages of his predecessors: for the Passion, especially Bonaventure, Alexander of Hales, Ubertino of Casale or Simon of Cassia; for the name of Jesus, his preference was Guibert of Tournai. Vast crowds gathered to hear him and, as we have said, his influence in spreading devotion to the name of Jesus was extraordinary.

4) With the simplicity and discretion of John Gerson can be contrasted the banality and truculence, the subtlety and farcical jesting, the mocking satire or the gloomy and vigorous terror of Oliver Maillard (†1502) and of other preachers of his time, although the evaluation of the oratorical genre of this Franciscan in the "macaronic" Latin that clothes his printed sermons calls for great prudence.

Let us recall to mind, nevertheless, that he preached the Passion at great length in the course of his Lenten sermons.

Maillard's sermons were dramas acted out in the pulpit of which he was an unparalleled producer. His dramatis personae were his contemporaries. If we confine ourselves to the Passion of Laval, the preacher described the actual crucifixion, the body of the dying Christ, the Virgin "kissing the bloodstained ground," and the descent from the cross in a realistic fashion as if he were contemplating one of those *Pietàs* that were so popular at the time.

c) Conclusion

These preachers were quite unassuming. Without recourse to much theology, they strove to teach the elementary data of faith and to attract their listeners to the person of Jesus. They did their best to put the Scripture texts and especially the gospels within everyone's reach, by "striving mainly to arouse our hearts to devotion," as Gerson states,[75] by translating the doctrine into easy, yet safe devotional practices that made it possible to attain a true "image and likeness of the Lord Jesus."[76] And so these preachers were primarily moralists and only secondarily apologists or satirists. They wanted to teach Christians how to live their faith in everyday reality. The methods were often sketchy and their aims somewhat short-sighted.

Let us be fair. There were not two kinds of preachers: those who gave moral, ascetical and satirical sermons, and those who taught *Life in Christ* as Nicholas Cabasilas († around 1373)[77] or mystical union as Tauler did. There was no clear-cut distinction between the two, although we have separated the two. They lived in one and the same religious climate, even if they addressed themselves to audiences of different human and Christian formation.

The same preacher could, moreover, speak in a different way
to different congregations. This was the case with Vincent
Ferrer and Peter d'Ailly whose spiritual writings we are acquainted with. This was also the case with Gerson's university
sermons and mystical treatises. Even in the *Sermon* analyzed
above, he ventures to grapple with the question of the "wonderful union of divinity and humanity" in Christ[78] and that of
interior prayer: "Let us now take the cross of Jesus on our
shoulders by holy recollection and devotion. Let us go with
Him outside the city by lofty contemplation. Let us always
bear in mind that we do not have any dwelling here until we
come to the everlasting mansion of paradise."[79]

Sermons, whether they were popular or scholarly, despite
appearances and in different ways, put the Christian on the
road to the imitation and love of Christ.

D. *From Devotion to Contemplation*

Devotion naturally leads to contemplation. This is the road
pointed out by the *Lives of Christ,* the *Meditations,* and the mystical experiences of the Middle Ages. "Carnal" love or "tender
devotion to the humanity of Christ," the devotion that "carnal"
minds pledge to him, gradually rises to spiritual love. This
spiritual love is nurtured by contemplation, and contemplation
could only lead to the imitation of Christ. Such is the very
simple road of the Christians who were taught by the medieval
spiritual authors. Félix Vernet has two beautiful chapters on
"the ascent to God" and "union with God" through Christ
in his book *Mediaeval Spirituality.* Acquaintance with the texts
perfectly corroborates his quick explanations and intuitions.

Through the act of devotion, through the devotional image,
one attains the inner or higher reality. By the acts, the words
and deeds of Jesus, by the picture that symbolizes Him to us,
through all that was associated with Him, by everything that
bears witness to His actual presence and action, we attain His
"interior" and this reality leads us to His Divinity. In His
turn, the God-Man becomes a "means," an "intermediary" between Himself and God, and the Trinity. This more or less
structured schema is found beginning with St. Anselm up to St.
Ignatius of Loyola. Neither the greatest vogue of devotions,

nor the time of "methodical exercises" or the trend of a "modern devotion" have warped it.

It is by degrees or by steps that we discover the *interior,* the *spiritual,* the God hidden in the God-Man, that we are led to the contemplation of the Trinity. This progressive method, as a matter of fact, consists first of all in applying the external senses to the images of the life of Christ, then in allowing each of our faculties to be purified and become saturated on contact with these images; this "contemplative rumination" ends in placing ourselves in the presence of the inner Christ. In this way we are led to imitate Him, to cling to Him, and to be transformed into Him.

There is some advantage to be gained by comparing the dates of composition and countries of origin of the works we are going to study. The majority of them were, as a matter of fact, written in the space of a century and a half, between the years 1300 for the *Meditations on the Life of Christ* and 1471, the date of Thomas à Kempis's death. The spiritual climate in which our authors lived was such that, without much risk of error, we can say that their doctrine and teaching were similar. And it would hardly be reasonable to dissociate asceticism from mysticism, devotion from contemplation, even if the emphasis was sometimes placed on devotion and "images," and at other times on "the interior man," on conformity and imitation of Christ and on what is beyond the image. There was continuity and harmony from one movement to the other. It was always a question of the same spiritual way, whether in one situation it was adapted to the beginner or in another to the cultured or more advanced Christian.

We can, nevertheless, distinguish different trends. In our treatment we will discuss first the Franciscan trend together with the *Meditations on the Life of Christ,* next feminine mysticism, then the German tradition with Henry Suso, John Tauler and the writings that are associated with them, and lastly, the "Devotio Moderna."

1. The Representations of Jesus Christ

The first steps that lead from devotion to contemplation are explained in a remarkable way by the pseudo-Bonaventurian *Meditations on the Life of Christ.*

a) Intention

The author addresses himself beyond the Poor Clares to "the uneducated and the simple,"[80] to beginners and the imperfect,[81] proposing a spiritual way to them that can guide them to the heights of perfection. His intention is to show that meditation on the life of Christ is the basis, the indispensable point of departure, the way *(fundamentum, via)* par excellence of every authentic Christian life—the classic Bonaventurian doctrine. The exercise that is set forth is, on the one hand, "the most necessary and the most profitable" to lead a virtuous Christian life and, on the other hand, to reach the spiritual life properly so-called, that it is to say, "to have time for God in intimate friendship with Him."

It is a matter of re-living the life of Christ as it is known through the texts of Scripture or the most authoritative witnesses —those of the saints, the mystics, the most reliable vestiges— or the most credible data. This recalling to mind, which is as detailed and prolonged as possible, by impressing itself on us "will inflame and quicken our hearts," which will then cling to the Lord and be drawn to imitate Him. It was in this way that St. Francis of Assisi became "as it were, a picture of Jesus" *(quasi pictura Jesu)*, even to the point of receiving the stigmata.

b) Method

The method depends on the audio-visual reconstruction, on the theatrical play, and the personal involvement.

All the senses participate in the audio-visual reconstruction: to see again what happened, to listen to what was said, and to acquire a taste for it, to familiarize oneself with the image that has been projected in this way into the memory, to return to it, to take it up again under new angles so that nothing escapes us. Better still, just as in a montage different things which are brought together to make an inseparable whole can be considered separately and together, so the author tries to consider Christ purely as a man,[82] then as God. This procedure, as we may well surmise, has its drawbacks. It is like a true scenario ready for the producer. Several passages are perhaps selections from mysteries; others in any case could, without much effort, become such.

But we are well beyond the visual animation and the "play." "The efficacy of the meditation lies completely elsewhere."[83] "Be present," the author tirelessly repeats, be present, greet, adore, genuflect, help Mary and the Child, travel with them, "share the sufferings of Jesus interiorly so that they may be your nourishmnt."[84] Why this "presence"? Because everything has been said, done, and suffered for us, for me.[85] Why then stress this "carnal meditation" if not because it is the surest way to avoid the "carnal life" and to arrive at "spiritual meditation."[86]

Note that all of this is expressed in a very limited vocabulary. A few words, always the same ones, without much contrast, suffice to express and to make what is most moving clear to a very simple public.

c) Meditation on the humanity of Christ

As a matter of fact, "meditation on what the Lord did in His flesh not only sweetly feeds the soul, but leads it to a stronger nourishment." It is "a ladder to reach contemplation in the spirit."[87]

The author leaves the Christian on the threshold of this contemplation. He is content with describing the active life and contemplative life by quoting many texts from St. Bernard. But he scarcely points out the purifying effect on the faculties of prolonged meditation on the humanity of Christ. It suffices for him to hint at it and to desire it. In seeing how the Lord acts with His mother, His apostles, His disciples, His friends, the crowds and with the people, we should come to a better understanding of how He acts with us *in a spiritual way (spiritualiter)*.[88] The Lord's life, His actions, and His words become intelligible to anyone who lives *spiritually (spiritualiter)*.[89]

It is in this way that the doctrine of the mediation of the humanity of Christ explains the meaning of the various devotions to Christ. Many of them result directly from the texts of the *Meditations*: the devotions to the Childhood, the Passion, the wounds, the blood, etc. Now it is worthy of note that this doctrine, this method and its aim, the devotions it suggests and the mediation that it seeks already belong to the teaching and experience of St. Bernard,[90] and that we find them again hardly developed any further, in the fourteenth and fifteenth centuries in the other *Lives of Christ,* in the spiritual treatises, in meditation books, even in Thomas à Kempis and St. Ignatius of Loyola. Doctrinal and devotional continuity in the Middle Ages is amazing.

d) Going beyond the image?

This type of meditation inevitably gives rise to a problem that cannot be overlooked: does not the activated imagination play an abnormal role in these fancied representations? Does it not, on the one hand, lead to psychological illusion and, on the other hand, to representations of the content of faith that are too "carnal"? We are not a little surprised to note that the Middle Ages were no less aware of this problem than we are. A short treatise by Gerard Groote (†1384) explains the *raison d'être*—the sense and limitations—of the image in meditation on the life of Christ. It is "because of the dullness of our eyes" that "Christ Himself taught in images." Therefore it is well to "make ourselves present," to picture the gospel personages to ourselves mentally, to speak to them, and to live with them. These images help us and are "signs," like the signs in regard to the sacraments, or a language, "what words are to the sciences." It is "impossible for a divine ray to reach us other than veiled in the wide range of what is perceptible by the senses," and the stronger the sensibly perceptible imprint is the stronger will the spiritual imprint be. It is nonetheless indispensable to purify our faculties and the images of our faith. Faith does not reside in the sensibly perceptible, even though the external senses introduce us to the spiritual senses; we must "go beyond the external signs," but not abandon them, "before the new Christ, the spiritual man, is formed in us." This takes place in the contemplation of the cross. St. Teresa's experience of the contemplation of the humanity of Christ will confirm in a convincing way these theological and spiritual views.

Written for the average Christian, the treatise of Groote is full of common sense and wisdom. It is one of the very rare essays of reflection on "images" in the Christian life of the Middle Ages.[91]

e) *Contemporaries*

To the Franciscan tradition to which the *Meditations on the Life of Christ* belong there belong also a goodly number of spiritual treatises that deserve to be examined. We shall limit ourselves to two of them which were contemporary with the *Meditations,* but very different in genre.

1) Were it not for its Joachimism (the reign of the Holy Spirit, the end of the world, and the "spiritual" Church) and its "enthusiasm," the *Tree of Jesus' Crucified Life* of Ubertino of Casale († around 1330) would merit our attention for its exceptional devotion to the Name and Heart of Jesus, and for its insistence on meditation on the life and Passion of Christ. But if Bernardine of Siena plagiarized Ubertino, it does not seem that the influence of the *Tree* went much beyond the Franciscan spiritual tradition.

2) Friar Rudolph of Biberach († 1350) in his anthology of patristic and medieval texts (up to the twelfth century) on the ascent of the soul in the "inner mystery and eternal abiding in Christ," gathers together first of all a few texts of Augustine and of Hugh of Saint-Victor which clearly show that the "humanity of Christ is the road that leads to his Divinity," or, in a more picturesque way, "from the pastures of His humanity one is led to the pastures of His divinity." The merit of these texts is to establish the continuity with tradition.

f) *The Life of Jesus Christ* of Ludolph of Saxony († 1378), a Dominican who entered the Carthusians around 1340, is to be compared with the *Meditations,* which it most often imitates. The success of these two works was so great that we may consider them as "the gospel" of Christians even beyond the sixteenth century. The *Life* has the same purpose, the same method, the same vocabulary, richer and more varied however, and the same approach to contemplation. The "frequent and assiduous meditation" on the life of Christ teaches us how "to be present" to Him, and is the only way that leads to *confidence* and *familiarity* with Him. In a word, this meditation is the only way to sanctity, because Christ, who always remains "the brightest mirror and model of all sanctity," is

the one and only way—and the Passion the *via regia* (the royal way), par excellence—that guides us toward the contemplation of God. Let us add that Ludolph, a contemporary of the Rhineland mystics, must have met Tauler and Suso at Strasbourg or Cologne and known their doctrine and writings.

Another Carthusian, Adolph of Essen (†1439), made extracts of the *Life* under the title of *Meditations,*[92] whereas the Franciscan John Brugman (†1473) composed some *Devote oefeninghe (Devout Meditations)* on the life of Christ by compiling the *Meditations* of pseudo-Bonaventure and the *Life* of Ludolph.[93]

2. Feminine Mysticism and the Humanity of Christ

Is feminine mysticism more human than masculine mysticism, less tempted by the darkness of the mind and of the heart? One might be led to think so, considering the attachment of the female spiritual authors to the humanity of Christ and in particular to His Passion, and their keen sensitivity to everything that pertains to the bodily sufferings of the Lord. Certainly, for them as well, Christ is the mediator of contemplation, but He is primarily the object of compassion and love, of veneration and "devotion." Gertrude and Mechtild blend liturgical life and personal devotions; Angela of Foligno fainted before the crucifix; Julian of Norwich saw in Christ a "mother"; and Catherine of Siena became inebriated with the blood of Christ.

a) There is a great sense of satisfaction in presenting the very feminine piety of St. Gertrude of Helfta (†1301/2). At the end of the thirteenth century, this cloistered nun, whose theological and spiritual doctrine is reliable and whose liturgical life was profound, prayed undoubtedly like many of her Sisters and many of the faithful. She narrates with great freedom the manifestations of her piety. Her devotions were spontaneous, concrete, familiar, affective, and truly typical, it would seem, of everyone. Gertrude harmonized them without any difficulty with her liturgical life. She knelt down for her personal prayers; she meditated on the Passion on Friday,[94] and desired to see the consecrated Host with her own eyes.[95] Her crucifix never left her; she showed a very lively devotion to it.[96]

Devotion to the Lord's wounds was something she was well acquainted with.[97] Her veneration of the Heart of Christ expressed her love and her mystical espousals. It was "through the infinitely meek Heart of Jesus Christ" that she devoutly recited the Office of the Blessed Mother.[98] Moreover, "her mystical life is a life of union with Mary and at the same time with Jesus."[99] She composed countless prayers to Christ, to whom she gave the most affectionate biblical names (O Jesus, my brother and spouse, great King, God and Lamb . . .).[100] One final point admirably expresses her comportment and spiritual life: she had the following prayer, which she herself undoubtedly composed, said for every day before a likeness of Christ crucified: "Through your wounded Heart, pierce, most loving Lord, her heart (Gertrude's) with the arrows of your love, to the point that it may no longer possess anything earthly, but that it be possessed by the sole power of your Divinity."[101]

b) St. Angela of Foligno (†1309) strove, first of all, to retain the Passion of Christ *in her memory.* She attended the Passion Play at Foligno in 1293;[102] she swooned before paintings of the Passion.[103] She asked "to pray in the life of the God-Man Jesus Christ, who is the book of life" in order to imitate Him, as Blessed Francis did.[104] She disclosed her teaching on "the way of the cross" and in particular on poverty.[105]

Next, she *experienced* the Passion, either because the crucified Christ appeared to her and revealed it to her or because He made her participate in His sufferings:[106] "My soul was transformed into sorrow, the likes of which I had never suffered."[107] The crucified Christ purified her in the blood from His side;[108] He engulfed her in His Passion and conformed her to Himself: "The more we see of the God-Man Jesus Christ the more we are transformed into Him through love and sorrow."[109]

Lastly, this assimilation filled her with an unspeakable *spiritual joy:* "There was not a day nor a night when I did not continuously have this joy from the humanity of Christ and the longing to sing some *laudi.*"[110] However, there came the day when she was "taken out *(extracta)* of the life and humanity of Christ" in order to enter into a state of light and knowledge concerning which one can only stammer. The Crucified One accompanied her, then, it seems, withdrew.[111]

   c) Regarding the mystical doctrine and experience of St. Catherine of Siena (†1380), we can in the framework of this study retain only one image, and one "devotion" which is more than a "devotion."

The crucified Christ is presented throughout her *Dialogues* as the *bridge* that necessarily connects Divinity and humanity.[112] This metaphor speaks for itself. After the ascension, we will pass by way of "the bridge of the doctrine of Christ crucified." *Bridge, door, way,* and *ladder* are all equivalent expressions. That is what the humanity of Christ is for the Christian. "I made a ladder of my body for you when I was nailed to the cross in order that you may lift yourself up."[113] From the "high table of the holy cross,"[114] the soul finds the wherewith to nourish itself with the bitterness and sufferings of Christ, and "in the sun of Christ crucified, it sees men and God."[115] "Having passed through the door of Christ crucified, it tastes the living water" in the Trinity.[116]

Catherine began many letters with this envoi: "In the name of Christ Jesus crucified and of sweet Mary . . . I write you and encourage you in His precious blood." For her the blood of Christ was everything: the redemption of love of Christ—"I have opened the door for you with my blood";[117] the bath of baptism—"recreated in blood,"[118] and of purification; but again the blood of Christ "inebriates, strengthens, sets us afire, and enlightens" us.[119] Grafted on to the tree of the most holy cross, "all the treasures of the Divinity will be opened to us and all His secrets will be revealed."[120]

3. From Purification to Perfect Union

For the Rhineland spiritual writers the method that leads the Christian from devotion to contemplation and from Christ's humanity to the Divinity seems to be rather simple, at least for Tauler and Suso, while the speculative Eckhart prefers to discourse on the spiritual birth of Christ in the soul.

   a) In the beginning the purpose of meditating on the life

and especially on the Passion of Christ was to become better acquainted with the redemptive plan and its fulfillment, to strive to *imitate* the exemplary actions and sentiments of Christ until He conformed us to Himself. "To follow in the footsteps of the Lord," "to enter into the divine Model by suffering with Him and imitating Him," is what Tauler demanded.[121] As for Suso, who certainly was not unacquainted with the pseudo-Bonaventurian *Meditations,* his approach is similar to theirs. On the day of the Presentation, for example, he ran in spirit ahead of the Blessed Virgin, knelt down before her, and begged her to stop; he received and contemplated the Child and sang a canticle to Him.[122] But he constantly longs: "Bring about in me the closest resemblance to your cross."[123]

Despite some mistrust of devotions that "keep us at the foot of the tree" and prevent us from climbing,[124] Tauler dedicated five sermons to the feast of the Exaltation of the Cross, while he manifests and favors a great devotion to the Blessed Sacrament.

b) The humanity of Christ, meditated upon in this way, is essentially considered as an *intermediary,* a "milieu," a way, "a royal way," a road, that leads to God, like a door that gives access to Him. Our authors repeat in many different ways that "the soul enters into God through union with the Passion of Christ."[125] They constantly stress the doctrine that has become classical since Augustine, namely, that the road to God necessarily passes through the humanity. "If you wish to contemplate me in my uncreated Divinity, you must learn to know me and to love me in my suffering humanity, for that is the quickest way to beatitude."[126]

By conforming us to His life and His sentiments, by regenerating us in His blood—and on that score He indeed deserves in some way to be called "Father"—Christ purifies us before ushering us into the divine Trinity. Christ's action and his spilt blood have as "their purpose to eradicate every trace of dissimilarity in us." As a matter of fact, the Passion has the power "to enlighten and purify" our faculties and our entire being.[127] It is by contemplating the Lord's wounds in the fire of love that this purification is especially brought about. Sin and the attraction to sin disappear as snow in fire: love con-

sumes them.[128] Following St. Bernard and William of Saint-
Thierry, the anonymous booklet *On Ten Forms of Blindness
(De Decem Caecitatibus)* (undoubtedly a "friend of God" addressing himself to "friends") links the purification of the
powers, conformity to the divine will, and union with God without any intermediary to each of the five wounds in an exercise
on the will of God. Tauler's sermon 79 ends with a very
similar exercise, although its structure is more measured. "Take
refuge with your ability to love in the divine Heart ... so that
He may draw you to Himself completely, both interiorly and
exteriorly, with all your faculties, and let all of this be done
through the holy and adorable wounds."[129] Complete renunciation, or radical poverty, our authors say, is the end result of
this purification. It is in this way that the humanity of Christ
calls the guests to the nuptials,[130] and that these "five sacred
wounds will remain open until the last day."[131]

    c) This purification of the powers disposes us to encoun-
ter God and to unite ourselves with Him, but *beyond images*—
"an image is a screen," Tauler says.[132] In fact, after "these
good exercises" of meditation and contemplation of the life
of Christ whose purpose is to inflame our *deep-seated will
(Gemüt),* it is advisable "to abandon these representations" and
to pass on into "the inner man" who remains purely passive
under God's action.[133] What does this mean? Tauler explains
himself. In the garden Mary Magdalene could no longer come
close to Christ "in a sensibly perceptible way, but only in the
way in which He is in the Father." And so, it is a question,
under the unique action of God, of purifying our images and
representations, of spiritualizing them, of making them resemble those which will be definitive in the "day of Jesus
Christ," and "to receive into ourselves the Passion and death
of the Lord more purely and more nobly, not in a tangible and
picturesque way, as our senses present them to us or as our
imagination pictures them to us, but interiorly and nobly, di-
vinely and mysteriously."[134] In this way Christ dead, risen, and
glorious, makes us climb by degrees to the most exalted mysteries."[135]

    d) Concerning Jan Van Ruysbroeck (†1381), we shall

restrict ourselves to the last part of *The Book of Twelve Beguines* on the "Passion of Christ divided into seven canonical hours."[136] The life and doctrine of Christ constitute "the book of hours common to the laity and clerics,"[137] which is to be recited and lived in a spirit of penance and imitation. Considerations on those who accept salvation and those who refuse it accompany the account of the Passion, which is sparsely commented on. Those who love "are baptized in the Holy Spirit and in the life-giving blood of our Lord with whom they live in God"; they are called to the contemplative life and to "essential love without images."[138] As for the reasonable man who clings close to virtue, "Christ lives in him by His grace and effects in him what is of precept as well as of counsel."[139] All are called, however, to "the heights beyond all modes: to transcend every created being in order to enter into the super-essence of the Divinity."[140]

e) Although he does not belong to the Rhineland-Flemish tradition, Richard Rolle (†1349) of Hampole deserves a moment of our attention. Specialists hesitate to rank this English hermit among the mystics, in the technical sense of the word; and yet he is one. He is an excellent representative of the English literature of the fourteenth century and a spiritual writer of distinction. "His devotion to Jesus," H. E. Allen acknowledges,[141] "is, as it were, the signature of all his writings." We met him when we were talking about the Name of Jesus, and his devotion to the blood of Christ is well-known. His *Meditations on the Passion,* addressed to the *Swete Lord Jhesu Cryst,* remind us somewhat of the pseudo-Bonaventurian *Meditations.* D. Knowles states that they are the best development in the English language on the subject and one of Rolle's masterpieces. From the purely descriptive point of view, no one, it seems, has surpassed them, so successful was he in guarding himself at one and the same time against a false sentimentalism, a realism devoid of sense, and an exaggerated symbolism.[142] This opinion is all the more important to point out since Rolle wrote this work as well as his others for his disciple, men and women, and for all those, whoever they are and wherever they are, who are concerned with leading an intense Christian life.[143]

It would be advisable, likewise, to consider here the poems in which Rolle praises Christ, but Rolle's devotion to and contemplation of the humanity of Christ have not yet been sufficiently studied.

4. With the Interior Master

a) The Imitation of Christ

Without in any way wishing to impose a plan on the four books that make up *The Imitation of Christ,* which began to circulate about 1424/27, we cannot but be struck by the central place given to Christ, to His life, His Passion, and especially to His cross, to the *Teacher of truth,* to the imitation of the Lord, to familiarity and intimacy with Him, to the entrance into the interior kingdom of the heart where Christ lives. "The soul enters into the intimacy of Jesus . . . it reaches the summit in love of the cross."[144]

It would seem that piety toward Christ becomes "more interior and more spiritual"[145] from one book to the other. It is all summed up in the following two desires: "We must make it our chief business to train our thoughts upon the life of Jesus Christ"[146] and "If you had once really entered into the mind of Jesus . . ."[147] Likewise, resignation, or abnegation and radical renunciation, which are its prerequisites, lead more and more clearly to pure love ("to love Jesus for His own sake," "to love Jesus purely, with no alloy of self-interest and self-love,"[148] "the man in love . . . gives all for all, [loves himself] only for your sake,"[149] "above all things and in all things"[150]). From one book to the other, the author, and the reader who is solicitous for the truth, practice self-renunciation, enrich themselves, emerge and rise under the promptings of grace, until "the inner self is remolded, until it takes on the likeness of God,"[151] to the point of complete abandonment and divine union.[152]

In a word, being closely associated with the historical Christ, having Him at his side at all times and yet transcending this experience, the author of the *Imitation* has set himself up on a higher level, that of spiritual presence, that of actual soliloquy and dialogue, in submissiveness to the inner Master.

We know that Book IV of the *Imitation* is entirely devoted to Eucharistic exercises: preparation for Communion and its reception, preparation for Mass and its celebration, and spiritual Communion. The latter is, moreover, linked much more closely to the life of Christ than to the Eucharistic banquet: "Every time you mystically communicate and are given that unseen refreshment, you devoutly recall the mystery of Christ's Incarnation and Passion; your heart is kindled with the fire of His love."[153]

b) Thomas à Kempis and the Devotio Moderna

Whether the *Imitation of Christ* belongs to Thomas à Kempis or whether it was composed in his milieu, we can no more isolate it from the doctrine of the *Devotio Moderna* than we can isolate the *Spiritual Exercises* of St. Ignatius from his principal works. To do so would be to set up a literary and spiritual "en soi," a work totally unrelated to anything else. It would make of it a book that is distorted, doctrinally fossilized, and undoubtedly impoverished.

In any case, we cannot fail to recall to mind the influence of the thought of St. Bernard, St. Bonaventure, of David of Augsburg, of the Rhineland school, and especially of Henry Suso on the doctrine of the *Imitation*. In reality, the *Imitation* was created in the climate of the *Devotio Moderna,* to which it owes its most profound characteristics.

It has perhaps not been sufficiently pointed out that the piety of the tradition of the *Devotio Moderna* did not know these manifestations of sentimental devotions which the artistic creations of the fifteenth century might lead us to suppose. No doubt there was a plethora of devotions offered to the world of clerics and the Christian people, but they are restrained, reasonable, tranquil, even dull and temperate—much more so than those of Henry Suso, for example—gesticulatory and concrete like all devotions, but not very spectacular, and in any case, interior. Their aim was to nurture and sustain everyday piety.

If the writings of Thomas à Kempis are in the same vein as the *Meditations on the Life of Christ,* they also reflect the spiritual climate of the *Imitation*.

The descriptions of the childhood of Jesus, for example, take up and develop the genre of pseudo-Bonaventure. The exhortation to "contemplate Christ as present" is realized in chapters 5-9 of the *Sermons* in a touching and spiritual way: "I shall remain here in the service of my Lord and of my lady holy Mary and of St. Joseph, your foster-father"; then follows the series of the small services rendered.[154] The meditation on the Passion is no less realistic, but it is more profound: veneration of the instruments of the Passion,[155] of the wounded members,[156] of the wounds and the blood shed;[157] fondness for the Seven Words, compassion for the Virgin, contemplation of the cross and of the Crucified One.[158] "I must not omit any detail," Thomas states very explicitly,[159] for "we must drill ourselves in the cross every day by meditation, reading and prayer."[160]

And yet we should not deceive ourselves. Why this contemplation of Christ? "To commiserate with Christ, to follow Him, imitate Him, and conform ourselves to Him,"[161] or "to instruct, inflame and purify,"[162] and lastly, to "glorify" the cross, for we cannot forget his extraordinary reflections on "the glorious cross," the instrument of salvation.[163] When the author steals into the stable among the shepherds and later with the Magi and peremptorily declares: "I, too, want to see, *volo ergo et ego videre,*" he hears the Child retort: "The eye of the heart is needed to see, the other is ordinarily harmful: he who believes in me sees me."[164] It is likewise "the inner eye of the heart that must be riveted on Jesus crucified,"[165] for the humanity of Christ alone gives access to the Divinity.[166]

Conclusion

It is obvious that the nutritive soil of devotion and contemplation of Christ's humanity at the close of the Middle Ages is without a doubt the doctrine of the Fathers and of the masters of the eleventh to the thirteenth centuries as well as the experience of the mystics. The spiritual relationship of St. Bernard to the *Meditation on the Life of Christ,* of St. Francis of Assisi to St. Angela of Foligno, of St. Bonaventure to Henry Suso, to the *Imitation* and to the *Devotio Moderna* is obvious.

At the same time we are obliged to note the evolution of mentalities and a clearer awareness of social and personal freedoms which necessarily have their repercussion on the concept of Christian life and the behavior of the faithful. This explains a more personal spiritual life as well as a more realistic piety. It was not disaffection with a communitarian liturgy—liturgical life, prayer, and personal devotions blend together very well, as Jean Leclercq has shown—with reading of the Bible, or a speculative theology, but rather a keener awareness of a God-Saviour who is also a man close to other men.

Briefly then, certainly by sometimes unexpected roads and not always fortunate methods—and this applies to the mystery plays as well as to the treatises of the mystics—everything contributes to help the Christian people cling to the Lord first in a more sensibly tangible way and then spiritually, to live in His materialized and then interiorized presence, and lastly to imitate Him "literally" in order to imitate Him better in all His being, briefly, to help Christians go from the image to the Image. "For by His glory, He is all that is great, being God, and by His mortal life He is all that is poor and abject. Therefore He has taken this unhappy condition, so that He could be all in all persons and the model of all conditions."[167]

Chapter V

The Carmelite School:
St. Teresa and St. John
of the Cross

by Tomas de la Cruz, O.C.D.

Around 1572, a graphic episode gives us a snapshot, as it were, of the characteristics of a Christological piety as it was lived daily in the school of St. Teresa and of St. John of the Cross. This episode took place, not in a Teresian Carmel, but in the old monastery of the Incarnation at Avila while the saints presided over its direction: Teresa as prioress, John of the Cross as confessor and spiritual director. We have a very short work by Teresa, *Answer to a Spiritual Challenge,* which scholars in general have overlooked and which tells us what happened. It was an answer to a spiritual challenge sent to the community of the Incarnation by the novices and the religious of the two Carmelite houses of Pastrana. John of the Cross had been there shortly before and had mitigated the ascetical excesses of the novice master. The purport of this challenge was to transport the knightly tournament into the domain of the monastic life.

The Avila community accepted the challenge; one by one the religious answered it by their own counter-challenge; and so did the prioress and the confessor, who disguised himself behind the name of "knight-errant." The answers were very brief, but replete with realism: snatches of their hard everyday life, sicknesses, temptations, sins, and difficulties were conjured up without human respect. The two saints let a hint of humor show through in their answer by alluding to the pseudo-virtues practiced by their adversaries. The ensemble clearly delineates the piety and the spiritual orientations introduced by the two saints into the monastery of the Incarnation: a simple Marian piety and especially a strong orientation toward Christ.

This last characteristic logically followed from the incentives that accompany the answers: "look at the crucifix three times a day in honor of the three hours which our Lord hung on the cross";[1] "consider the poverty in which Jesus Christ was born and died";[2] "keep company with the Lord for the three hours that He was on the cross";[3] ask for grace each day "through the torment He suffered when He was being nailed to the cross";[4] take part in "what the Virgin experienced at the foot of the cross."[5] Other basic aspirations likewise to be found in this work are: the service of Christ and perseverance,[6] love of Christ,[7] and the grace to serve Jesus Christ.[8]

The value of this short work lies in its direct witness. It documents for us the situation and the spiritual climate of a community guided by the two saints. The secondary devotions, including devotion to St. Joseph which is so Teresian, are absent. Christ is central and even the evocations of the Virgin have their *raison d'être* only in Him. Among the mysteries of Christ, His birth and especially His death on the cross take first place. The Eucharistic theme does not appear until Teresa's answer, that is, in no. 28. This work does not help us to grasp the doctrine that basically underlies and gives meaning to the very concrete piety which it expresses, but it does document the efficacy and deep-rootedness of the teaching of the two masters.

A. St. Teresa of Avila (†1582)

The vigor with which Teresa of Avila took a stand, and a doctrinal stand at that, on the subject of Christ's humanity[9] was decisive for the Carmelite school. Her position laid the foundations and explains the fact that the saint's influence was more immediate and more determinative than that of John of the Cross, despite the greater substance and depth of John's doctrine. Teresa's thought follows a trajectory that is easy to plot: a) as a starting point, she has her own internal experience which serves as a support and point of reference for her entire teaching; b) in her description of the beginnings and the development of the spiritual life, Christ the man intervenes with His mysteries, His person, and His teaching; the mysteries of His human life are both the object and source of knowledge and love; His person is the Friend we are seeking to encounter, and His love will be the very essence of the interior life; lastly, He is the Master who teaches; c) as we make our way into the interior of this mystery, these christological motifs, which are more or less limited and subjective, become all-embracing: Christ is absolutely the way, the truth, and the life; and His presence is the key to the enigma of the life of the perfect.

1. St. Teresa's experience develops from her first steps to capture the historical Christ of the gospel up to the mystical penetration of the presence of Christ in the mystery of the Christian life. These two stages are strongly emphasized. To what extent she familiarized herself with the Christ of the gospels is not easy to ascertain. She certainly read and assiduously meditated upon the *Life of Christ*[10] of Ludolph the Carthusian. She also made use, but to a lesser degree, of the *Imitation of Jesus Christ,* of Francis of Osuna, Bernardino of Laredo, and Louis of Granada. The christological instructions of the Carmelite Rule made an impression on her only quite late in life.

On the other hand, the *Libro de su vida* shows us in a concrete way how her prayer was directed to Christ. In reality, Teresa prayed in order to reach Christ, to enter into contact with Him, and to fathom personally the events of His life. She sought the person of the Lord in His humanity; she needed concrete situations and circumstances: the conversation with the Samaritan woman,[11] His friendship with Magdalene,[12] His entrance into Jerusalem,[13] the Last Supper with His disciples,[14] His communal life with them,[15] and especially the salient moments of His Passion; she needed to meet Him alone in the garden of Gethsemani,[16] in His agony,[17] in the scenes of the *Ecce Homo,* especially His flagellation and His presentation to the people.[18] She was unable to picture to herself the episodes and concrete environment that historically surround these mysteries.[19] She strove to interiorize them in her prayer in order to achieve a true, human encounter with Christ the man. In fact, she failed, and she did not succeed in living these encounters to the depths she needed. In one circumstance she did indeed live the scene of the *Ecce Homo* with such intensity that it brought about her conversion.[20] What she needed was to be introduced into the experience of Christ by an entirely different road, the mystical road; it would not estrange her from the historical Christ, but would usher her into the mystery of Christ present in the Church and in herself. This experience was given her by surprise; in an altogether unexpected way, she discovered Christ present at her side.[21] Without any sensory element, she was given the pure perception of His presence; He was there. Later on, this presence became specific and enriched by this or that aspect of the humanity of Christ,[22] of His Sacrament,[23] and of His glorious existence.[24] The mystical presence of Christ in the life of the saint established itself in a permanent way: "Jesus Christ seemed to me to be always walking at my side."[25] That presence especially determined the last stages of her spiritual ascent. In truth, the entrance into the seventh mansion—the consummation of the spiritual journey—took place in a crowning experience of the humanity of Christ, the authentic "sacrament of (mystical) consummation."[26] In short, the saint was subjected to an experience of the mystery of Christ in His humanity from the very elementary beginnings of exterior imitation and meditative reflection up to her discovery and enjoyment of Him interiorly at the heart of the mystery of salvation.

2. *The common teaching* of the saint on the humanity of the Saviour and His role in the spiritual life is in part the doctrinal version of her own experience. This did not permit her to enter deeply into the theology of baptism (see however her *Letter* 38.1). She found it increasingly important to actualize the episodes of Christ's life and to become personally acquainted with them in order to be able to live them. For example, she enunciates a principle when she writes:

> This method of prayer which consists in remaining in the company of Christ is beneficial to all states; it is the

surest means of making progress in the first degree of
prayer, of reaching the second in a short time, and of
advancing with security in the last ones. . . .[27] We know
that to please God we must follow the Commandments
and the counsels . . . meditate on the life and death of
the Lord and on all that we owe Him.[28]

In her analysis of the components of the Christian life—the
virtues, degrees, graces, offices in the Church—Christ is the
unit of measurement and the point of reference.

All this appears more clearly in the main emphasis of
Teresa's spirituality, prayer. The *Way of Perfection* is centered
on the commentary of the *Our Father*,[29] the Lord's own prayer,
His efficacious word to keep Him present and active in our own
conversation with the Father. A pedagogy of Christian prayer
grows out of this basic concept. One by one the seven petitions
are used to discover the Master's sentiments, to lay hold of
them, and to utilize them as our own in our conversation with
the Father. In this way the doctrinal exposition decreases,
giving way to lively developments: the author adheres to
Christ's prayer and prays with Him; she introduces the reader
into her own sentiments and brings it about that he prays with
her; Teresa and her reader cling to Christ, pray with Him
by entering into His sentiments in order to lift themselves up
to the Father.

3. The summit of the saint's teaching is reached when she
considers from the summit of the mystical life the close relationship that exists between Christ's humanity and Christian
life. Her thought is recorded in two polemic chapters, perhaps
the most vigorous and the most explicit of any the saint has
written: *Life,* chap. 22, and *Interior Castle* 6, chap. 7. In these
chapters, her own personal experience and doctrinal interpretation are again intermingled. "I had been so devoted to Christ
throughout my whole life!"[30] However, at the halfway mark
of her life, she fell into a painful error: she wanted to set
Christ's humanity aside in order to rise to a higher contemplation of the divine.[31] Despite the apparent affinity of this view
to certain teachings of the *alumbrados* (the name given to
sixteenth-century Spaniards who adhered to illuminism), the

saint's attitude was not in any way connected with them. Her error was to be laid first of all to certain spiritual books she was using,[32] then to the theologians who were counseling her.[33]

Without being aware of it, through her reading Teresa had entered into contact with an old spiritual tradition that went back to Neoplatonism and to pseudo-Dionysius: to aspire to the highest spiritualization of the Christian life by transcending everything corporeal in order to achieve even in this life the purest contemplation of God.

In all probability, the books to which she alludes belonged to authors of the new Spanish Franciscan school, perhaps Francis of Osuna or Bernardino of Laredo, but more surely Barnabas of Palma, the author of the *Via spiritus o de la perfección espiritual del anima*.[34] It is easy to find in this book the sentences corresponding to the presentation that St. Teresa makes of them.[35] If Barnabas was not a first-rate author, he nevertheless commanded Teresa's attention.

Barnabas did not take the trouble to cite his authorities. However this may be, Teresa accepted the book's injunctions and put them into practice. She had already been initiated into the early forms of mystical contemplation; she had discovered and experienced the formidable mystery of the divine presence.[36] In order to immerse herself in it and abandon herself to the unfathomable depths of the Divinity, she tried to put aside everything corporeal and, consequently, to go beyond Christ's humanity.[37] The result was the opposite of what she expected. The tone with which she reports this experience is one of painful bitterness: "I cannot recall this opinion (she had first written: 'error') to mind without a feeling of pain; it seems to me that it was a great betrayal on my part, even though I did it in ignorance."[38]

The saint drew a profound doctrinal lesson from this experience. We may summarize her thought in this way:

   a) Christ's humanity is never an obstacle to the Christian life; there is no time in the forward march of the interior life when recourse to the life and mysteries of Christ hinders penetration into the sphere of the divine.[39]

b) On the contrary, the Lord's holy humanity is the door and the road to all grace,[40] and this is true not only in the ontological order ("I desire no good if it is not acquired from Him from whom comes all good"[41]), but also in the contemplative order; faith and contemplation of the mysteries of the Lord are the indispensable channel for rising to the divine.[42]

c) Christ's humanity is the object of the contemplation of the perfect, including the highest degrees in the mystical life, as the saint notes in the seventh book of the *Mansions*; at these heights, the mysteries of Christ will be reached in a very pure and wonderful way, "where both his divine and human companionship is ever present";[43] if these mysteries are not the sole object of the contemplation of the perfect—sometimes they give way to more exalted mysteries: the divine attributes, God, or the Trinity[44]—nevertheless the texture of the highest state of the Christian life is constituted by the twofold causal and objective presence of the holy humanity.[45]

Lastly, one question has been raised indirectly which later drew the attention of the Teresian school and led it to re-evaluate the Dionysian doctrine: do the most exalted acts of contemplation within the highest state of the perfect have as their exclusive object the divine Being or not? In the *Life*[46] the saint does not deal with this subtlety, and of course offers no solution to it.

Thus, Teresa took a position on a delicate point of spiritual theology. She did not intend to offer refinements regarding a subtle problem of specialists, but to safeguard the Christological nature of the Christian life in all its dimensions: the full presence and action (not only in the ontological, causal order) of Christ's humanity are the highest expression of the mystery of salvation wrought in each Christian.

B. St. John of the Cross (†1591)

St. John of the Cross made a substantial contribution to Teresa's teaching on the above theme more than on any other.

Despite the profound differences in their respective points of view, it is undeniable that the two teachers understood each other and mutually accepted each other, not only in the domain of practice (cult, exercises, etc.), but also on the plane of doctrine. Teresa taught John and she made use of him.[47] For his part, John of the Cross thought highly of her[48] and praised her teaching.[49] Teresa, in turn, in one of her humorous passages,[50] cleverly stresses one of the points on which their doctrines on the Lord's humanity contrast and seem to conflict, as we shall see.

It is certain that in John's synthesis Christ's humanity offers a clearly different profile from the one given by Teresa. It has been observed that Teresa's Christ is much closer to that of the Synoptics, whereas John's Christ is closer to the Gospel of St. John and to St. Paul.[51] We should remember Teresa's predilection for the historical facts of Christ's life. On the contrary, John of the Cross prefers chapter seventeen of St. John and the Pauline Christology, including Hebrews 1. This explains why the Lord's humanity is less prominent at first sight and why, on the other hand, John's Christology, his vision of Christ in the mystery of the divine unity, and his reducing the mystical union to the prototype of the hypostatic union are more profound. This depth makes the presentation of John's doctrine of the humanity of Christ somewhat difficult.

1. Let us begin with *experience.* Here John of the Cross differs greatly from Teresa. There is even a greater difference in their respective ways of reporting their experience. A few episodes from John's life will suffice to define his spiritual attitude toward Christ's humanity. Some of them deal with acts of a very personal love before the crucifix; he himself carved crucifixes out of wood and gave some of them away. We know that several of these acts result from deep mystical graces. After having received one of these graces, when he was confessor at the monastery of the Incarnation, he took a pen in hand and sketched in broad outlines the famous "crucifix of St. John of the Cross." His most touching poem, *El Pastorcico,* is also the result of a few strokes of the pen that revised some strophes which were originally secular and made them evoke Christ the Shepherd who ascends the cross to die on it. Perhaps behind the lyrical expression there was a grace. As is evident, the themes of the incidents we have related are centered around the Paschal Mystery, more precisely around Christ's death on the cross. The content of the *Romances* is less unified, and

other themes are introduced: the Incarnation, the birth of
Christ, and the Eucharist. We know from other sources the
intense affection with which the saint staged the celebration of
the Nativity. Lastly, his powerful poem, the *Spiritual Canticle,*
gathers together and assembles a series of personal, authentic
experiences with Christ the Beloved Spouse which are not related to the schemata of the two mysteries of the Incarnation
and Easter; and yet the purpose of these experiences is the presence of Christ in the mystery of salvation as the poet lived it.
The same thing holds for the "Prayer of the Soul in Love," which
culminates in the experience of the possession of Christ as the
most precious of all created goods: "Mine are the heavens
and mine is the earth . . . the Mother of God and all things are
mine, and even God is mine and for me because Christ is
mine. . . ."[52]

2. The saint's experience already enables us to catch a
glimpse of what his *Christological synthesis* will be. This synthesis does not restrict itself to the schema God-Man, nor does
it seek a balance between the Paschal Mystery and that of the
Incarnation. It is concerned with the total mystery of Christ
which in the divine economy is the center and fullness, whether
it is a question of the history of salvation, of the reality of
the Church, or of the Christian life of each individual. In God's
dialogue with man, Christ is the Word, the final and definitive
Word of the Father in whom He has said everything.[53] Once
He has said it, "God has remained, as it were, mute, and has
no more to say."[54] The plan of salvation is complete in Christ:
the hypostatic union is the model of our union with God in
which the holiness of the Church as well as that of every Christian is brought about.[55] To imitate Christ is the norm of the
Christian life and "the road to all spiritual good."[56] Union with
God—holiness—is union with Christ. By Him and with Him
the return to the Trinity is brought about.[57]

In this framework, it is rare that Christ's humanity is considered for itself; neither His actions, His traits, nor even the
history of His life, or the human element of Christ's mystery
is underscored. But the mysteries of His humanity, the deep
"veins" that it concealed are: "There are great depths to be
fathomed in Christ because He is like a rich mine that has

作者：蔣承贊　　　　　　Painter:Chiang Cheng-Tsan

在世界上你們要受苦難；
然而你們放心，我已經戰
勝了世界。

約十六：三三

That in me you may find peace. You will suffer in the world. But
take courage! I have over come the world.

(John 16:33)

numerous recesses containing treasures which men are ever digging without being able to exhaust them. On the contrary, in each recess men go on discovering new veins, with new riches everywhere."[58] All the beauty *(hermosura)* of creation is reflected and recapitulated in Him: "My Beloved, the mountains, the valleys . . . the streams." But two mysteries dominate all the others: the Incarnation and especially the cross.

The Incarnation is viewed, not as self-abasement, but as the triumphal entrance of Christ into creation and as the uplifting of the latter.[59] At the center of this mystery, the hypostatic union is also the secret key to our spiritual life, which is consummated in the union of the soul with God.

In the Paschal Mystery, John of the Cross places great emphasis on the cross. He bases one of the essential elements of his teaching, namely, absolute "negation," on the death of Christ. The Lord's death postulates our own. This accounts for the radicalism of this doctrine of the negative way: the death, the self-abasement of the soul in the sensual and spiritual realms must correspond to the death of Christ so that it may be united to Him. This is summed up in the *Ascent*:

> At the moment of His death, Christ was annihilated in His soul and was deprived of any consolation and relief, since His Father left Him in the most intense aridity. . . . This was the greatest desolation that He had suffered in the lower part of His nature during His stay on earth . . . at the moment and time when this Lord was most completely annihilated in everything, namely, with respect to the esteem of man . . . with respect to nature, because by dying He annihilated Himself in it; with respect to the protection and spiritual consolation of the Father, since at that time He abandoned Him . . . reduced, as it were, to nothing."[60]

To this spiritual vision of the mystery of the cross there corresponds the negative aspect of the Christian life:

> God said this so that the truly spiritual man may understand the mystery of the gate and of the way of Christ, in order to be united with God, and may know that the

more completely he is annihilated for God's sake, according to these two parts, the sensual and the spiritual, the more completely he is united to God . . . And when he comes to be reduced to nothing . . . then the spiritual union between the soul and God will be brought about . . . (The latter) does not consist in refreshment, in consolations, or in spiritual feelings, but in a living death of the cross, both as to sense and as to spirit.[61]

To know Christ is to enter into the depths of this mystery, into the knowledge of the cross.

3. This doctrine of John of the Cross, which he brought to its ultimate conclusions in the purification of the mind (the dark night), poses questions. To what extent does the purification of the created forms and means compel the mind to *renounce considering the humanity of Christ?* The radicalism of "nothing" and of the "nights" demands a freedom of the mind and a transcending every means disproportionate to the Divinity; if one wants union with God, he must dismiss everything that is less than God, therefore every creature. Contemplation in pure faith, obscure and indistinct knowledge cannot be achieved by images, memories, or limited forms and concepts.

Here we again find the problem posed by Teresa: among corporeal things (John of the Cross, being more radical, would have used the word 'creatures'), will the humanity of Christ be an inadequate road and door to lift up the soul to the highest summit of the Christian life? Is John's night a version of the Dionysian darkness? Does it end in sending us back to the old doctrine of Neoplatonism? Does the highly spiritual union with the divine exclude, not the ontological influence of Christ's humanity, but indeed the content of His mysteries from the contemplative act of the perfect?

Starting from opposite points of view, J. Baruzi[62] and K. Rahner[63] have called attention to this implication of John's doctrine: it is a theological, but not a Christic mysticism. Authors have not failed to note likewise the absence of Christ in John's nights. The soul that goes through them conjures up the prototypes of David, Job, certain prophets of the Old Testament, but not Jesus Christ. Hence a twofold suspicion arises: is this not a symptom that the experience of the night as lived by the author was a void and absence of Christ? Is it not the proof that this absence is postulated by the system?

It is true that the radical purification demanded by the saint imposes the elimination of certain sensorial and human forms of adherence to the Passion of Christ and to the human side of His mystery.[64] Nevertheless, two things are evident: on the one hand, at the time the saint was experiencing the nights, he composed the *Spiritual Canticle,* his strongest testimony of his experience of the Beloved. On the other hand, in the last phase of the mystical life, "the state of the perfect,"[65] these latter are allowed to enter into the breadth and depths of the mysteries of Christ, the "God-Man," including those which are rooted in His holy humanity.[66] The final union of the soul is celebrated with Christ the Bridegroom and the Incarnate Word. The purification will bring it about that the mysteries of His holy humanity will be attained with "very enlightened faith" in so pure and spiritualized a manner that this humanity of Christ will indeed be the road and the door to the equality of love with the Trinity.

C. The Disciples

1. The two saints by their visits to the first Spanish houses marked them with their *Christological* piety, with a very definite orientation toward the Lord's humanity. In this environment, numerous legends, similar to the *Fioretti,* sprang up, particularly concerning the Infant Jesus and His presence in Teresa's mystical life. A number of these legends are related to the statues of the Infant which she gave to her daughters. The importance of images in the Spanish piety of the sixteenth century is well known; Teresa was a representative of this form of popular piety. Likewise a few statues and representations of the *Ecce Homo* and of the Crucified One, connected with the crucial moments of her life, have been preserved.[67] But in particular, very simple statues of the Infant Jesus are preserved in every Carmel founded by the saint. Around them there sprang up dramatic representations of the mysteries of the Childhood which took place during the liturgical seasons of

Advent and Christmas. John of the Cross had already begun to do this.

Devotion to the Infant assumed distinctive forms in the Carmels, in particular that of the Infant Jesus of Prague which associates the themes of childhood and of royalty.[68]

In line with this piety, let us also note a series of poems called *villancicos* or canticles in honor of the Virgin Mary, like those which the two saints composed. Those of James of Jesus are very restrained and very refined. There are some similar to them in the manuscripts of the Carmels of Madrid and Florence.

2. Writings of Spiritual Formation

The first systematic attempts at a pedagogy of piety toward Christ appeared in the Carmelite houses of formation.   In her *Instrucción de novicias* (around 1588) Mary of Saint Joseph made an attempt of this kind in the form of a delightful dialogue among the novices of Lisbon in which all of them take their turn expressing their sentiments on the Lord's Passion. This was the first stage of a method that the most gifted Italian Carmelite spiritual master, John of Jesus and Mary, born in Calahorra, developed to a very great extent. His claim to fame lies in the fact that he envisioned that pedagogy of piety toward Christ on a practical plane, that he did so with much finesse, and that he nourished it with the inspiration and the contents of Scripture.

The greater part of his lesser writings was composed for Italian novitiates with a view to nourishing interior life there in an immediate, direct way; thus, for example, his *Anagogical Letters* addressed to Christ, a series of rather similar elevations that complete his *Art of Loving God,* the *Soliloquies to Jesus Christ. The School of Jesus Christ* has a more doctrinal cast, just as the *Incentive to Compunction,* especially chapters 22-33.

Jerome Gratian (†1614), for his part, wrote treatises of a moralizing and catechetical tone, particularly chapters 2-20 of his *Vida del alma* and his *Sumario de las devociones.* Thomas of Jesus (1564-1627) developed in a very deep and theological way the progress of devotion to Christ, from spiritual initiation up to mysticism; he has, nevertheless, in the line of practical piety, a short treatise: *Práctica de la viva fe de que el justo vive.*

Many other Carmelite authors made use of this vein in their writings; we have mentioned only the most representative ones. The influence of John of Jesus and Mary in the school was profound and definitive, even though, as a matter of fact, he represented only the Teresian tradition, as did Mary of St. Joseph and Gratian. His pedagogical orientation profoundly stamped the style and Christological content of later Carmelite spirituality.

3. In the domain of *spiritual doctrine,* two facts were decisive for the Carmelite school: Teresa's position in favor of the role of Christ's humanity at all the degrees of the spiritual life and especially at the highest degrees of the mystical life, and the apparent divergent position of John of the Cross when he applies his doctrine of purification and of emptiness to the highest degrees of contemplation and union. The treatises of mystical theology and the great *Cursus* of the seventeenth and eighteenth centuries tend to remain faithful to the two masters and to make their teachings agree, with, however, more fidelity to Teresa than to John. Their theological constructions, on the other hand, undergo a twofold pressure in the opposite direction, the tradition of quietism and that of the influence of Dionysius. The first was constantly combatted, in obedience to the magisterium of the Church. It contained errors similar to those that Teresa denounced.[69] The traditional Dionysian trend reserved a contemplation in "the ray of darkness" to the perfect, without any admixture or connivance of the corporeal and the sensual, and harmonized the positions of John of the Cross regarding the night and the purification of every image, form, and distinct knowledge *(noticias).*

a) We have an example of the collision of Teresian mysticism with different positions in Jerome Gratian's polemics against the spiritual writers of the Low Countries. In his *Apología contra algunos que ponen la suma perfección en la oración unitiva immediata con aniquilación . . .* the sixth proposition, according to which "meditation and knowledge of God by creatures, and all the exercises of the internal and external

senses, and all the intellectual operations of the soul, and all
other things perceptible by the senses or the mind are imperfect
and must be abandoned . . ." was an attack against Teresa's doctrine. Gratian defended her doctrine (second part), without
renouncing the Dionysian doctrine (third part), but by attack-
ing Germanic theology. This *Apología* is an appendix to *La
vida del alma, libro que trata de la imitación de Cristo,* which
sets forth the same doctrine.

b) Within the Carmelite school, the divergence of the two
masters on the subject of Christ's humanity was quickly grasped
by certain of their disciples. An example of this would be
Quiroga's *Apología mística en defensa de la contemplación
divina* . . . especially chapter 16: "How to bring the memory
of Christ's humanity into play in contemplation without im-
peding the principal effects of contemplation." In this chapter, the author answers the accusation brought against John of
the Cross by comparing his doctrine with Teresa's in chapter
seven of the *Sixth Mansion.*

More recently, the introduction of Mary of the Blessed Sacrament to the *Writings* of St. John of the Cross underscores
this divergence.

But Teresa's famous passages[70] which set forth her teaching
on Christ's humanity and His presence in the entire course of
the spiritual life are the ones most generally studied and
quoted as solid doctrine and beyond discussion. Let us cite
Mary of St. Joseph in her *Instrucción de novicias,* Quiroga
in a short, manuscript treatise, *Declaración del c. 22 del Libro
de la Vida de nuestra santa madre Teresa,* and all the outstanding authors of the school up to Joseph of the Holy Spirit,
the Andalusian.

On the other hand, when an edition of the writings of John
of the Cross was finally published,[71] the editor who was responsible interpolated or revised certain important passages.
He had a twofold purpose in doing so: that of making the doctrinal concordance of John and Teresa more evident and, secondly, of avoiding probable denunciations of the saint's ortho-
doxy under the pretext of illuminism. In short, let us say that
the editor, as far as the general doctrine of the purification is
concerned by which the saint excludes everything corporeal

and every distinct form, introduced an exception in favor of Christ's humanity and did so with expressions based on those of Teresa's texts. In so doing, he ran the risk of deforming one of the essential areas of St. John's doctrine.

The principal mutilated passages which treat our subject are: a) *Ascent* II, chapter 32, 4: the interpolation of a long paragraph. b) *Ascent* III, chapter 2, 14: the mutilation of the original text and interpolation with strong Teresian overtones. c) *Dark Night* I, chapter 10, 6: interpolation. d) Another addition, short but symptomatic—here underlined in the quotation below—occurs in *Ascent* III, chapter 15, 1: "The more the soul dispossesses the memory of forms and of things it may recall to mind that are neither God *nor the God-Man whose memory is always helpful to the end, since He is the true way and guide and author of all good,* the more it will set its memory upon God . . ."

These four altered passages were pointed out by one of the persons responsible for the first edition, James of Jesus of Salamanca. The edition includes his *Apuntamientos y advertencias* whose purpose is to explain and defend the edited writings. He refers the reader to the four passages we mentioned above at the end of his second discourse.

Despite the precarious situation of the authentic doctrine of St. John on the precise point of the role of Christ's humanity, the Carmelite authors of the seventeenth and eighteenth centuries have in general succeeded in maintaining a balanced position. They affirm the Teresian doctrine and the traditional Dionysian doctrine. This last asserted itself, thanks to Gratian, to Thomas of Jesus and, closer to us, beginning with Quiroga. According to the Carmelite school, in the highest act of contemplation, every object that is not the Divinity is excluded. Yet, the influence of the presence of Christ's humanity, in the ontological causal sense, is constant. However, according to this view, the humanity of Christ is not the object of the most perfect act of contemplation.

We should note that in the eighteenth century Joseph of the Holy Spirit, the Andalusian, returned to a more radically Teresian position of affirming the constant presence of Christ's humanity as both the ontological cause and the object of contemplation.

Notes*

NOTES TO THE PREFACE

[1] C. H. Dodd, *The Founder of Christianity* (London, 1971); J. Guillet, *The Consciousness of Christ* (Staten Island, New York, 1972); J. Jeremias, *New Testament Theology*, Volume One: *The Proclamation of Jesus* (London, 1971). See also the two beautiful books of R. Aron, which reflect upon the childhood of Jesus in the light of the Jewish practices of His times: *Jesus of Nazareth: the Hidden Years* (New York, 1962); *The Jewish Jesus* (Maryknoll, N.Y., 1971).

[2] Vatican II, *Constitution on the Sacred Liturgy*, no. 7.

[3] See M. Ivens, "The Dimensions of Group Prayer," *The Way*, Supplement no. 16 (Summer, 1972), 67-79.

[4] Vatican II, *Dogmatic Constitution on Divine Revelation*, no. 12.

NOTES TO CHAPTER 1

[1] Oscar Cullmann, *The Christology of the New Testament* (Philadelphia, 1963), 137.

[2] Ibid., 138-188.

[3] Pliny the Younger, *Letters* 10.96.

[4] Arnobius, *The Case against the Pagans* 1.36.

---

* Since this series is intended for English readers only, many references in the original articles of the DS to publications in foreign languages have been omitted. All titles of primary sources have been translated into their English equivalents. When quotations from secondary sources are given in the body of the text, reference is made in the footnotes to the book or article from which the translation has been made.

⁵ Clement of Alexandria, *Christ the Educator* 3.

⁶ Cullmann, op. cit., 137.

⁷ Many texts are cited by J. Lebreton in *Histoire du dogme de la Trinité, des origines au concile de Nicée*, 2 (Paris, 1928), 201-242.

⁸ *Didache* 9.4 and Clement of Rome, *Epistle to the Corinthians* 20.11.

⁹ Origen, *Prayer* 15.

¹⁰ *Martyrdom of Polycarp* 1 and passim; the Letter of the Churches of Vienne and Lyons in Eusebius, *Ecclesiastical History* 5.1.41.

¹¹ Ignatius of Antioch, *Rom.* 6.3.

¹² *Martyrdom of Polycarp* 9.3.

¹³ See Barnabas, *Letter* 5, and Clement, *Epistle to the Corinthians* 16.

¹⁴ See Justin, *Dialogue with Trypho* 86-114.

¹⁵ Ignatius, Polycarp, and later Tertullian, *On the Flesh of Christ* 6, PL 1:809. This will remain a classical theme; see, for example, St. Basil, *Letters* 261; St. Leo, *Sermons* 64 and 65.2.

¹⁶ Irenaeus, *Against Heresies* 3.4.2.

¹⁷ See M. Frost, "*Te Deum laudamus*, The Received Text," *Journal of Theological Studies*, 33 (1943), 59-68; 193.

¹⁸ Irenaeus, *op. cit.*, 3.22.1-2; Hippolytus, *Against All Heresies*.

¹⁹ Irenaeus, op. cit., 1.10.1.

²⁰ See DS, vol. 7, col. 552.

²¹ See M. Harl, *Origène et la Fonction révélatrice due Verbe incarné* (Paris 1958), 258-261.

²² Ibid., 338.

²³ Ibid., 154-157.

²⁴ See F. Bertrand, *Mystique de Jésus chez Origène*, Théologie 23 (Paris, 1951), passim and 143-146.

²⁵ Harl, op. cit., 287.

²⁶ Origen, *Homilies on Luke* 18.

²⁷ Ibid., 15.

²⁸ Origen, *Commentary on John* 22.6.

²⁹ H. de Lubac, introduction to *Origène. Homélies sur la Genèse*, SC 7, 27-28; numerous references in F. Bertrand, op. cit., 147.

³⁰ Augustine, *Homilies on the Gospel of John*.

³¹ John Chrysostom, *Homilies on St. John's Gospel* 31.3.

³² Titus of Bosra, *Sermon for Palm Sunday* 7.

³³ DS, vol. 4, cols. 653-654.

³⁴ Ambrose, *Exposition of Luke's Gospel* 10.56-62.

³⁵ Ibid., 10.68.

³⁶ Ibid., 6.33.

³⁷ Augustine, *On the Psalms* 58.2.

[38] Ibid., 61.4.

[39] Augustine, *Questions on the Gospels* 38.

[40] Athanasius, *Concerning the Incarnation and Against the Arians* 3 and 22.

[41] DS, vol. 4, col. 1707.

[42] John Chrysostom, *Homilies on St. John's Gospel* 88.3.

[43] Augustine, *On the Psalms* 21.1.

[44] Ibid., 118.27.

[45] DS, vol 2, cols. 2617-2618.

[46] DS, vol. 7, cols. 1820-1831.

[47] DS, vol. 3, cols. 26-33.

[48] DS, vol. 6, col. 726.

[49] For Jerusalem, see art. "Chemin de la Croix," DS, vol. 2, cols. 2577-2578; for Bethlehem, see art. "Crêche," ibid., cols. 2421-2522.

[50] John of Damascus, *The Orthodox Faith* 3.8.

[51] Ibid., 4.11.

NOTES TO CHAPTER 2

[1] DS, vol. 2, cols. 1673-1716.

[2] Ibid., cols. 1643-2193.

[3] Origen, *Against Celsus* 3.59.

[4] Origen, *Homilies on Numbers* 10.3.

[5] Origen, *Commentary on Matthew* 17.

[6] Origen, *Homilies on Numbers* 27.12.

[7] Origen, *Commentary on John* 2.29.

[8] Origen, *Commentary on Ezechiel* 6.10.

[9] Ibid.

[10] Origen, *Homilies on Genesis* 7.

[11] Origen, *Commentary on Matthew* 12.30.

[12] Ibid., 14.7.

[13] Ibid., 1.18.

[14] Origen, *Commentary on the Song of Songs* 1.

[15] A. Lieske, "Die Theologie des Christusmystik Gregors von Nyssa," *Zeitschrift für katholische Theologie,* 70 (1948), 56.

[16] DS, vol. 2, cols. 1872-1885.

[17] J. Daniélou, *Platonisme et théologie mystique,* 2nd ed. (Paris, 1954).

[18] See DS, vol. 6, cols. 988-1003.

[19] W. Völker, *Gregor von Nyssa als Mystiker* (Wiesbaden, 1955), 184 and 216; 162-224.

[20] Gregory of Nyssa, *Homily on the Sixth Beatitude.*

[21] Lieske, op. cit., 64.

22 Gregory of Nyssa, *Homilies on the Song of Songs* 10.
23 Ibid., 3.
24 Ibid., 4.
25 Ibid., 8.
26 Gregory of Nyssa, *Life of Moses.*
27 Völker, op. cit., 214. For the bibliography on Gregory, see DS, vol. 6, cols. 1008-1011.
28 A. Harnack, *Précis de l'histoire des dogmes* (Paris, 1893), 269.
29 Augustine, *Confessions* 1.11.17.
30 Ibid., 3.4.8.
31 Ibid., 3.6.10; 5.3.5.
32 Ibid., 5.14.25.
33 Ibid., 7.20.26.
34 Ibid., 7.18.24.
35 Ibid., 7.21.27.
36 Ibid.. 7.18.24.
37 Ibid., 10.43.68-70.
38 Ibid., 4.10.20.
39 Ibid., 7.19.25.
40 Augustine, *Sermons* 92.3.
41 Augustine, *The Trinity* 13.19.25.
42 Ibid., 15.14.23; *Homilies on the Gospel of John* 29.3.
43 Augustine, *Letters* 137.2.8; 137.3.9.
44 Augustine, *Admonition and Grace* 11.30.
45 Augustine, *The Trinity* 13.17.22.
46 Augustine, *Confessions* 10.43.68.
47 Harnack, op. cit., 269.
48 Augustine, *The Trinity* 13.19.24.
49 Augustine, *On the Catechizing of the Uninstructed* 22.40.
50 Izid., 4.7-8; *Confessions* 7.21.27; *The Trinity* 13.17.22.
51 Augustine, *Homilies on the First Letter of John* 7-8.
52 Augustine, *Confessions* 10.43.69.
53 Augustine, *Homilies on the First Letter of John* 6.13.
54 See *Miscellanea agostiniana* (Rome, 1930), 453.
55 Augustine, *On Psalm 42*, passim.
56 Augustine, *The Trinity* 1.8.16.
57 J. M. LeBlond, *Les conversions de saint Augustin* (Paris, 1950), 237.

NOTES TO CHAPTER 3

1 E.g. Bernard, *Sermon 43 on the Song of Songs.*
2 William of Saint-Thierry, *On Contemplating God* 11.82.
3 Rupert of Deutz, *On the Divine Liturgy*, prologue.

⁴ See J. Leclercq, DS, vol. 2, col. 1936.

⁵ These texts have been published by C. Plummer, *Irish Litanies* (London, 1925).

⁶ See Paul Warnefred, "In Regulam S. Benedicti," *Biblioteca Casinensis*, 4 (Monte Cassino, 1880), 52.

⁷ See Jean Leclercq and François Vandenbroucke, *The Spirituality of the Middle Ages* (London, 1968).

⁸ DS, vol. 6, cols. 1175-1176.

⁹ U. Berlière, *L'ascèse bénédictine des origines à la fin du 12ᵉ siècle* (Paris, 1961), 83: "... to know the majesty of God, the goodness and mercy which He showed in the Incarnation of the Divine Word ... the infinite love of the Word made flesh, the greatness and role of the Virgin Mary, the dignity of the Church, the Spouse of Christ."

¹⁰ William of Saint-Thierry, *The Golden Epistle to the Carthusians of Mont Dieu.*

¹¹ William of Saint-Thierry, *Commentary on the Song of Songs* 16 and 18.

¹² William of Saint-Thierry, *Meditations* 10.

¹³ William of Saint-Thierry, *On Contemplating God* 10.

¹⁴ Ibid., 11.

¹⁵ Bernard, *Sermon 43 on the Song of Songs; On Contemplation* 5.7-12.

¹⁶ E.g. *Letters* 107.8 and the sermons for the vigil of Christmas.

¹⁷ See Bernard, *The Steps of Humility.*

¹⁸ See Bernard, *On the Love of God.*

¹⁹ See Bernard, *Sermon 20 on the Song of Songs; Sermons* 28. 9-10; this is a commentary on "Do not touch me" (Jn. 20:27); the sermons for the Ascension.

²⁰ See Bernard, *Sermons on Different Subjects* 87.

²¹ Aelred, *The Mirror of Charity* 3.516.

²² See DS, vol. 6, cols. 331-339.

²³ Thomas Aquinas, *Summa theologiae*, 2ª2ᵃᵉ, q. 82, a. 3.

²⁴ See DS, vol. 5, cols. 1271-1303.

²⁵ A. Sepinski, *La psychologie du Christ chez S. Bonaventure* (Paris, 1948), 233-234.

²⁶ See DS, vol. 1, col. 1841.

²⁷ DS, vol. 1, col. 714.

²⁸ J. P. Grausem, "Le *De contemplatione* du chartreux Guigues du Pont," RAM, 10 (1929), 259-289; see also DS, vol. 6, cols. 1176-1179.

NOTES TO CHAPTER 4

¹ See above, chapter 1.

[2] See DS, vol. 3, cols. 238-239.

[3] Félix Vernet, *Mediaeval Spirituality* (London and St. Louis, 1930).

[4] Ibid.

[5] See DS, vol. 1, cols. 225-234; vol. 5. col. 658.

[6] G. Cohen, *Mystères et Moralités. Manuscrit 617 de Chantilly* (Paris, 1920), cxliv.

[7] *Meditations on the Life of Christ*, chap. 1.

[8] St. Ignatius, *Spiritual Exercises* 102.

[9] G. Duby, *Fondements d'un nouvel humanisme, 1280-1440* (Paris, 1966), 152, 164.

[10] Ibid., 124-125.

[11] Ibid., 166.

[12] Ibid., 78.

[13] Ibid., 89-90.

[14] Ibid., 30.

[15] Etienne Delaruelle in Fliche-Martin, 14 (Paris, 1964), 606.

[16] See DS, vol. 7, col. 1016.

[17] The first three letters of the name of Jesus in Greek, which in the Latin tradition were mistaken for an acronym meaning *Jesus Hominum Salvator* (Jesus Savior of Men).

[18] E. Longpré, "S. Bernardin de Sienne et le nom de Jésus," *Archivum historicum franciscanum*, 29 (1936), 153.

[19] See DS, vol. 6, col. 1163.

[20] A. Wilmart, *Le "Jubilus" dit de saint Bernard* (Rome, 1944), 242.

[21] See also *The Chastising of God's Children*, ed. J. Bazire and E. Colledge (Oxford, 1957).

[22] Julian of Norwich, *The Revelations of Divine Love*, ed. James Walsh, in the present series. See also DS, vol. 3, cols. 770-771, and Paul Molinari, *Julian of Norwich: The Teaching of a 14th Century Mystic* (London, 1958).

[23] On the preceding section, see the articles "Crêche," DS, vol. 2, cols. 2520-2526; "Dévotions," vol. 3, cols. 766-771; "Enfance de Jésus," vol. 4, cols. 656-665.

[24] See art. "Crosiers," DS, vol. 2, cols. 2564-2572.

[25] Bonaventure, *Holiness of Life* 6.

[26] From Bonaventure, Thomas Aquinas, and Hugh of Strasbourg up to Henry Suso, Thomas à Kempis, Gerson, and Bernardine of Siena, the Passion of Christ is considered to be in all respects more painful than the sufferings ever endured by anyone.

[27] E. Gilson, "Saint Bonaventure et l'iconographie de la Passion," *Revue d'histoire franciscaine*, 1 (1924), 413.

[28] Bernard, *On the Song of Songs* 61.7-8.

William of Saint-Thierry, *Meditations* 11.

[30] John Tauler, *Sermons* 66.

[31] J. Toussaert, *Le sentiment religieux en Flandre à la fin du moyen âge* (Paris, 1963), 266-267.

[32] See in the DS the articles "Coeur (Sacré)," "Croix (Chemin de la croix; Mystère de la croix)," "Douleurs (Notre-Dame des Sept)," "Eucharistie (Dévotion eucharistique)," "Face (Sainte)." On the Clocks and Offices of the Passion, see DS, vol. 7, cols. 752-754.

[33] Paul Thoby, *Le Crucifix, des origines au moyen âge* (Nantes, 1959), with a preface by M. Aubert.

[34] M. Aubert in Thoby, op. cit., x.

[35] Ibid., 194.

[36] Ibid., 177.

[37] Ibid., 178-179.

[38] Bonaventure, *Great Legend* 14.4.

[39] Gilson, op. cit. (note 27), 418

[40] M. Aubert in Thoby, op. cit. (note 33), xiii.

[41] Henry Suso, *The Life of the Servant* 4 and 45; *Little Book of Letters* 11 and the work's greetings and maxims; *The Wisdom Clock*, 2nd pt., chap. 7.

[42] Henry Suso, *The Life of the Servant* 13; see DS, vol. 2, cols. 2603 and 2606.

[43] Henry Suso, *The Life of the Servant* 23.

[44] Henry Suso, *Little Book of Eternal Wisdom*, 3rd pt.

[45] B. Lauvard, *L'oeuvre mystique d'Henri Suso*, 1 (Paris, 1946), 21. See DS, vol. 6, col. 225, and vol. 2, cols. 2602-2603.

[46] Henry Suso, *The Life of the Servant*, chap. 16; see chap. 7.

[47] André Wilmart, "Le grand poème bonaventurien sur les sept paroles du Christ en croix," *Revue bénédictine*, 47 (1935), 262.

[48] DS, vol. 3, cols. 755-760.

[49] J. Bazire and E. Colledge, eds., *The Chastising of God's Children* (Oxford, 1957), 71-72. The original dates from about 1400.

[50] See in the DS the articles: "Frères," vol. 5, cols. 1205, 1208, 1213; "Génuflexions," vol. 6, cols. 213-226; Books of "Heures," vol. 7, cols. 411-416, 429-431.

[51] G. Cohen, "Anthologie du drame liturgique en France au moyen âge," *Lex Orandi*, 19 (Paris, 1955), 260.

[52] L. Petit de Julleville, *Les mystères*, 1 (Paris, 1880), 6.

[53] See art. "Flagellants," DS, vol. 5, cols. 392-408.

[54] See DS, vol. 5, cols. 400-401.

[55] Vincent Ferrer, *Sermons* 66.

[56] Ibid., 166.

[57] Ibid., 47.

[58] Ibid., 76.

[59] Ibid., 19.

[60] Ibid., 74.

[61] Vincent Ferrer, *Dominicale* 70.

[62] Vincent Ferrer, *Sermons* 35; *Quadragesimale* 2.

[63] Vincent Ferrer, *Dominicale* 56.

[64] Ibid., 34.

[65] John Gerson, *Sermon on the Passion,* ed. G. Frénaud (Paris, 1947), xv.

[66] Ibid., 31.

[67] Ibid., 48.

[68] Ibid., 7.

[69] Ibid., 10.

[70] Ibid., 99.

[71] Ibid., 29.

[72] Ibid., 99.

[73] Ibid., 93.

[74] Ibid., 119.

[75] Ibid., 7.

[76] Ibid., 31.

[77] See DS, vol. 2, cols. 1-9.

[78] John Gerson, *Sermon on the Passion,* ed. G. Frénaud (Paris, 1947), 30.

[79] Ibid., 74.

[80] *Meditations on the Life of Christ,* Prologue.

[81] Ibid., chap. 50.

[82] Ibid., chap. 77.

[83] Ibid., chap. 9.

[84] Ibid., chap. 77.

[85] Ibid., chaps. 15, 35, 96, etc.

[86] Ibid., chap. 99.

[87] Ibid., chap. 99.

[88] Ibid., chaps. 35 and 36.

[89] Ibid., chaps. 38 and 43.

[90] E.g., Bernard, *On the Song of Songs* 20.6-7.

[91] See DS, vol. 6, col. 27; vol. 7, cols. 723-725.

[92] See DS, vol. 1, cols. 209-210.

[93] See DS, vol 1, cols. 1967.

[94] Gertrude, *The Life and Revelations* 3.39, 54.

[95] Ibid., 3.18.

[96] Ibid., 2.41-45.

[97] Ibid., 2.4; 3.47.

[98] Ibid., 3.46.

[99] Gertrude, *The Exercises.*

[100] Ibid., 3.281.

101 Ibid., 2.5.

102 Angela of Foligno, *The Book of Divine Consolation* 66.

103 Ibid., 21.

104 Ibid., 130-132.

105 Ibid., 161-163; 174-179.

106 Ibid., 40, 64, 127-129, 135, 141, 151.

107 Ibid., 70-74, 112.

108 Ibid., 17.

109 Ibid., 132, 140.

110 Ibid., 107, 112.

111 Ibid., 119, 121.

112 Catherine of Siena, *Dialogue*, chaps. 21-30, 53-56.

113 Catherine of Siena, *Letters* 76.

114 Ibid.

115 Catherine of Siena, *Dialogue*, chap. 96.

116 Ibid., chap. 54.

117 Ibid., chap. 100.

118 Ibid., chaps. 4, 30, passim.

119 Catherine of Siena, *Letters* 25.

120 Catherine of Siena, *Dialogue*, chap. 75. For Saint Bridget of Sweden († 1373), see DS, vol. 1, cols. 1943-1958; Blessed Dorothy of Montau († 1394), vol. 4, cols. 1664-1668; Saint Clare of Assisi († 1253), vol. 5, cols. 1401-1409; Saint Colette of Corbia († 1447), ibid., cols. 1412-1415; Hadewijch (13th century), vol. 7, cols. 13-23.

121 John Tauler, *Sermons* 61.

122 Henry Suso, *The Life of the Servant*, chap. 10. See *The Little Book of Eternal Wisdom*, chap. 18; *Sermons* 3.

123 Henry Suso, *The Little Book*, chap. 18.

124 John Tauler, *Sermons* 45.

125 Henry Suso, *The Life of the Servant*, chap. 53.

126 Henry Suso, *The Little Book*, chap. 1; John Tauler, *Sermons* 64.

127 John Tauler, *Imitation of the Poor Life*, 2nd pt., chap. 7.

128 Ibid., 1st pt., chap. 9.

129 John Tauler, *Sermons* 54.

130 John Tauler, *Exercises or Meditations*, chap. 49.

131 John Tauler, *Sermons* 54.

132 Ibid., 6.

133 Ibid., 66.

134 Ibid., 76; see 65.

135 Henry Suso, *The Clock of Wisdom*, chap. 2.

136 Jan van Ruysbroeck, *The Book of Twelve Beguines;* French translation in *Oeuvres* (Brussels and Paris, 1937), 197-259.

137 Ibid., chap. 71.
138 Ibid., chap. 77.
139 Ibid., chap. 78.
140 Ibid., chap. 81.
141 Richard Rolle, *English Writings* (Oxford and New York 1931), xxiii.
142 See D. Knowles, *The English Mystical Tradition* (London, 1961, 64.
143 See ibid., 53.
144 P. Debongnie, "Les thèmes de l'Imitation," *Revue d'histoire ecclésiastique*, 36 (1940), 317.
145 Ibid., 319-320.
146 *The Imitation of Christ* 1.1.
147 Ibid., 2.1.
148 Ibid., 2.11.
149 Ibid., 3.5.
150 Ibid., 3.21.
151 Ibid., 3.54.
152 Debognie, op. cit. (note 144), 324.
153 *The Imitation of Christ* 4.10.32.
154 Thomas à Kempis, *Sermons on the Lord's Life and Passion*, chap. 7.
155 Thomas à Kempis, *Prayers and Meditations on the Life of Christ* 2, chap. 17.
156 Ibid., 1, chap. 34.
157 Ibid., 1, chaps. 19 and 32; 2, chaps. 16 and 21.
158 Thomas à Kempis, *Sermons on the Lord's Life and Passion*, chaps. 22-26.
159 Ibid., chap. 21.
160 Ibid., chap. 23.
161 Ibid., chaps. 22 and 25.
162 Ibid., chap. 26.
163 Thomas à Kempis, *Sermon 23*.
164 Thomas à Kempis, Sermons..., chap. 9. This echoes "to believe in Christ is to perceive with the mind," ibid., chap. 2.
165 Ibid., chap. 21.
166 Ibid., chaps. 21 and 8.
167 Pascal, *Pensées* 785.

NOTES TO CHAPTER 5

1 Teresa, *Answer to a Spiritual Challenge* 8. The writings of Teresa are cited according to the edition of Silvero de Santa Teresa, *Obras de santa Teresa de Jesús*, 9 vols. (Burgos, 1915-1924). The English reader can consult *The Complete Works of St. Theresa,*

trans. and ed. E. Allison Peers, 3 vols. (London, 1946).

[2] Ibid., 10.

[3] Ibid., 11.

[4] Ibid., 22; see 23.

[5] Ibid., 20 and 27.

[6] Ibid., 16.

[7] Ibid., 17.

[8] Ibid., 22.

[9] Teresa, *Life*, chap. 22; *Interior Castle* 6.7.

[10] Ludolph of Saxony, *Vita Christi*, ed. of Seville, 1538.

[11] Teresa, *Life*, chap. 30.19; *Way of Perfection*, chap. 19.2; *Conceptions of the Love of God*, chap. 7.6.

[12] Teresa, *Life*, chaps. 9.2; 22.9 and 12; *Spiritual Relations* 42; *Way of Perfection*, chap. 34.7.

[13] Theresa. *Spiritual Relations* 26.

[14] Teresa, *Way of Perfection*, chap. 42.1.

[15] Teresa, *Life*, chap. 26.6; *Interior Castle* 5.4.7.

[16] Teresa, *Life*, chaps. 9.3-4; 29.4.

[17] Ibid., chaps. 22.5; 27.13.

[18] Ibid., chaps. 10.2; 13.12 and 22; *Way of Perfection*, chap. 26.5; *Interior Castle* 4.1 and 6.

[19] Teresa, *Life*, *chaps.* 4.7; 9.6; *Way of Perfection*, chap. 26.2.

[20] Teresa, *Life*, chap. 9.1.

[21] Ibid., chap. 27.2.

[22] Ibid., chap. 28.1-3.

[23] Teresa, *Spiritual Relations* 15 and 26.

[24] Teresa, *Life*, chaps. 28.3 and 8; 29.4.

[25] Ibid., chaps. 27.2 and 29.2.

[26] Teresa, *Interior Castle*, 7.2.1-3.

[27] Teresa, *Life*, chap. 12.3.

[28] Teresa, *Interior* Castle 6.7.9.

[29] Teresa, *Way of Perfection*, chaps. 22-42.

[30] Teresa, *Life*, chap. 22.4.

[31] Ibid., chap. 22.3.

[32] Ibid., chap. 22.1 and 3.

[33] Ibid., chap. 22.8; *Interior Castle* 6.7.5.

[34] This work was published in Salamanca in 1541.

[35] Teresa, *Life*, chap. 22.1.

[36] Ibid., chap. 18.15.

[37] Ibid., chap. 22.2.

[38] Ibid., chap. 22.3.

[39] Ibid., chap., 22.4-5; *Interior Castle* 6.7.5-6 and 8.

[40] Teresa, *Interior Castle* 6.7.8.

[41] Ibid., 15.

[42] Teresa, *Life*, chap. 22.6-7.

[43] Ibid., chap. 22.9 and 11.

[44] Ibid., chap. 22.9.

[45] Ibid., chap. 22.6.

[46] Ibid., chap. 22.8-9.

[47] Teresa, *Foundations*, chaps. 10.4; 13.5; see also her *Letters*.

[48] John of the Cross, *Letters* 1.1. The writings of John of the Cross are cited according to the edition of Simeon de la Sagrada Familia, *Obras*... (Burgos, 1959). The English reader can consult *The Works of St. John of the Cross*, trans. and ed. E. Allison Peers, 3 vols. (London 1953).

[49] John of the Cross, *Spiritual Canticle* 13.7.

[50] Teresa, *The Veil* 6.

[51] Jean de la Croix Peters, "Función de Cristo en la mistica," *Revista de espiritualidad*, 17 (1958), 511.

[52] Compare Jn 17 and 1 Cor 3:22-23 with *Ascent* 3.35.5 and *Spiritual Canticle* 36.5.

[53] See *Ascent* 2.22 with the initial citation from Heb 1:1.

[54] Ibid., 2.22.4.

[55] See *Spiritual Canticle* 37.3.

[56] John of the Cross, *Ascent* 2.29.2; see *Counsels* 2.

[57] See the last strophes of the *Spiritual Canticle*.

[58] John of the Cross, *Spiritual Canticle* 37.5.

[59] Ibid., 5.4.

[60] John of the Cross, *Ascent* 2.7.11.

[61] Ibid.

[62] J. Baruzi, *Saint Jean de la Croix et le problème de l'expérience mystique* (Paris, 1931), 548, 646-647.

[63] K. Rahner, "The Eternal Significance of the Humanity of Jesus for Our Relationship with God" in his *Theological Investigations*, 3 (Baltimore, 1967), 35-46 .

[64] John of the Cross, *Ascent* 2.12.3.

[65] John of the Cross, *Spiritual Canticle* 36.1 and 37.1ff.

[66] Ibid., 37.2-4.

[67] See Teresa, *Life*, chap. 9.1.

[68] See art. "Enfance de Jésus," DS, vol. 4, esp. cols. 664-665, 667-668, 676-677.

[69] Teresa, *Life*, chap. 22.

[70] Ibid.; see also *Interior Castle* 6.7.

[71] In Alcala, in 1618.

BIBLIOGRAPHY

Chapter 1   *Primary Sources*

The Apostolic Fathers. FC 1.

Arnobius, *The Case against the Pagans.* ACW 7.

Augustine, *Homilies on the Gospel of John.* NPNF, 1st ser., vol. 7.

————, *On the Psalms.* ACW 29 and 30.

Basil, *Letters.* FC 28.

Clement of Alexandria, *Christ The Educator.* FC 23.

Egeria, *Diary of a Pilgrimage.* ACW 38.

Eusebius, *Ecclesiastical History.* 1 FC 19.

Hippolytus, *The Refutation of All Heresies,* ANF 5.

Irenaeus, *Against Heresies.* ANF 1.

John Chrysostom, *Homilies on St. John's Gospel.* FC 33 and 41.

John of Damascus, *The Orthodox Faith.* FC 37.

Origen, *Prayer.* ACW 19.

Pliny the Younger, *Letters.* Loeb Classical Library.

Saint Justin Martyr. FC 6.

Secondary Sources

Cullmann, O., *The Christology of the New Testament.* Philadelphia: 1963.

Frost, M., "*Te Deum Laudamus,* the Received Text," *Journal of Theological Studies,* 33 (1943), 59-68.

Chapter 2   *Primary Sources*

Augustine, *Confessions.* FC 21.

————, *Homilies on the Gospel of John; Homilies on the First Epistle of John.* NPNF, 1st ser., vol. 7.

————, *Letters.* FC 18.

————, *On the Catechizing of the Uninstructed.* NPNF, 1st ser., vol. 3.

————, *On Admonition and Grace.* FC 2.

————, *The Trinity.* FC 45.

Gregory of Nyssa, *The Beatitudes.* ACW 18.

Origen, *Commentary on John.* ANF 10.

————, *Commentary on John.* ANCL vol. 9.

————, *Commentary on Matthew.* Ibid.

————, *Contra Celsum.* Cambridge: 1935.

————, *The Song of Songs, Commentary and Homilies.* ACW 26.

Chapter 3   *Primary Sources*

Bernard, *Letters.* Chicago: 1953.

————, *On the Love of God.* New York: 1937.

————, *On the Song of Songs.* CF 4.

―――, *Sermons on the Canticle of Canticles.* Dublin: 1920.

―――, *The Steps of Humility.* Notre Dame: 1963.

―――, *Treatises,* I. CF 1.

―――, *Works.* London: 1889.

Bonaventure, *Itinerarium Mentis in Deum.* St. Bonaventure, New York: 1956.

Thomas Aquinas, *Summa Theologiae.* 2nd ed. New York: 1912-1936.

William of Saint-Thierry, *Exposition on the Song of Songs.* CF 6.

―――, *The Golden Epistle.* CF 12.

―――, *On Contemplating God, Prayer, Meditations.* CF 3.

Secondary Sources

Bouyer, L., *The Cistercian Heritage.* Westminster, Md.: 1958.

Leclercq, J., and Vandenbroucke, F., *The Spirituality of the Middle Ages.* London: 1968.

Plummer, C., *Irish Litanies.* London: 1925.

Chapter 4   *Primary Sources*

Angela of Foligno, *The Book of Divine Consolation.* New York: 1909.

Bernard, *On the Song of Songs,* CF 4.

―――, *Sermons on the Canticle of Canticles.* Dublin: 1920.

Bonaventure, *Holiness of Life.* St. Louis: 1923.

―――, *The Life of St. Francis.* London: 1904.

―――, *The Mysticel Vine. Fleur de lys* 5. London: 1955.

Catherine of Siena, *Dialogue.* London: 1896.

The Chastising of God's Children, ed. J. Bazire and E. Colledge. Oxford: 1957.

The Exemplar. Life and Writings of Bl. Henry Suso, O.P. Dubuque: 1962.

Gertrude, *The Exercises of St. Gertrude.* Westminster, Md.: 1960.

―――, *The Life and Revelations.* Westminster, Md.: 1949.

Ignatius of Loyola, *The Spiritual Exercises.* Chicago: 1952.

Imitation of Christ. New York: 1959.

Julian of Norwich. *The Revelations of Divine Love.* Ed. James Walsh, vol. 3 in the present series.

Pascal, *The Provincial Letters, Pensées, Scientific Treatises.* Great Books of the Western World 33. Chicago, London, Toronto: 1952.

Pseudo-Bonaventure, *The Minor of the Blessed Life of Jesus Christ.* London: 1926

Rolle, Richard, *English Writings.* Oxford and New York: 1931.

Signposts of Perfection. A Selection from the Sermons of Johann

Tauler. St. Louis and London: 1958.

Tauler, John, *Spiritual Conferences*. St. Louis: 1961.

William of Saint-Thierry, *Meditations*. London and New York: 1954.

Secondary Sources

Knowles, D., *The English Mystical Tradition*. London: 1960.

Molinari, P., *Julian of Norwich: the Teaching of a 14th Century Mystic*. London: 1958.

Vernet, F., *Mediaeval Spirituality*. London and St. Louis: 1930.

Chapter 5   *Primary Sources*

The Complete Works of St. Theresa. 3 vols. London: 1946.
The Works of St. John of the Cross. 3 vols. London: 1953.

Secondary Sources

Rahner, K., "The Eternal Significance of the Humanity of Jesus for Our Relationship with God," *Theological Investigations*. Vol. 3. Baltimore: 1967.